The Incomplete Revolution

THE INCOMPLETE REVOLUTION

Adapting to Women's New Roles

Gøsta Esping-Andersen

polity

First published in 2009 by Polity Press

Polity Press
65 Bridge Street
Cambridge CB2 1UR, UK

Polity Press
350 Main Street
Malden, MA 02148, USA

ISBN-13: 978-0-7456-4315-1
ISBN-13: 978-0-7456-4316-8 (pb)

A catalogue record for this book is available from the British Library.

Typeset in 11 on 13 pt Berling
by Servis Filmsetting Ltd, Stockport, Cheshire
Printed and bound by MPG Books Group, UK

The publisher has used its best endeavours to ensure that the URLs for external websites referred to in this book are correct and active at the time of going to press. However, the publisher has no responsibility for the websites and can make no guarantee that a site will remain live or that the content is or will remain appropriate.

Every effort has been made to trace all copyright holders, but if any have been inadvertently overlooked the publishers will be pleased to include any necessary credits in any subsequent reprint or edition.

For further information on Polity, visit our website: www.polity.co.uk

Contents

Illustrations

Acknowledgements

Some years ago I solemnly promised to myself that I would from then on dedicate my research and writing to anything but the welfare state. And here I am at it, once again. It all sprang from one of those offers that you cannot refuse. At the end of 2006, the Collège de France bestowed upon me the honour of giving the annual 'Trois Leçons'. In lieu of the ongoing, and certainly intense, debates on the future of social protection in France, I could not but design the three lectures around social policy questions. The lectures were converted into a slim book, *Trois Leçons sur L'Etat de Providence*, published by Le Seuil in 2008. I used the same three lectures as blueprints for chapters 3–5 in this new book, but found that they required substantial revision and supplementary evidence. The French versions were written primarily for a general, non-specialized audience; the English version aims to be more scholarly.

To be honest, being unfaithful to my solemn promise came easy. My supposedly 'post-welfare state' work has been hovering around issues related to intergenerational mobility, equality of opportunities, family demography and the changing contours of social and economic inequality. It does not take much imagination to see the centrality of such questions for social policy.

One issue that in particular reunited me with the welfare state has been social inheritance in general, but especially the impact of early childhood conditions on later life chances. The search for the true mechanisms that explain life chances led me inevitably to think about how we might forge policies to secure the best chances for all children. In fact, I have found myself trotting in the footsteps of James Heckman on a campaign to enlighten the world to the urgency and centrality of investing in our children. To my surprise, I was met with many receptive audiences in politics and in academia. I would in particular like to thank Ruud de Mooij, Paul Nyrup Rasmussen, the people at the IPPR, the EU Presidency and Bruno Pallier for pushing me to campaign for babies. I would also like to thank those who invited me to do the campaigning: the Belgian presidency of the EU, the NETSPAR and the Social Insurance Institute in the Netherlands, the IPPR in Britain, The University of Southern Denmark, Aalborg University, the Danish Parliament, the French and German Socialist Parties, the Swedish Embassy in Berlin, the Max Planck Institute for Demographic Studies, the Catalan government, the Spanish Ministry of Finance, the EU's Social Policy Advisory Board and, not least, the Collège de France.

My research over the past years has found its way into the chapters that follow and, thanks to so many excellent research assistants, many of the empirical findings are, I think, interesting and scientifically on solid ground. I remain hugely indebted to Josep Mestres (who worked with me on the IALS and PISA data); Stefanie Brodmann (who ran thousands of fertility regressions); Berkay Ozcan (who wrestled with all the thorny methodological problems of identifying how women's work affects the income distribution); and Pablo Gracia (who, like Stefanie, is now running thousands of time-use regressions). And not to forget, all this research could evolve only thanks to the generous funding from the Spanish Ministry for Education and Science (Research Grant SEJ 62684).

I have also been helped along by my colleagues, many of whom are also friends. I am hugely indebted to Bruno Pallier for his role in facilitating the 'Trois Leçons' project, from which the idea of this book emerged. I have learned a lot about time-use research from Jens Bonke, and John Myles is always there to bring me down to earth and continues to be one of my favourite co-authors. Chapter 5 in this book is an outgrowth of an earlier paper he and I wrote some years ago. I also owe thanks to Marco Albertini, Lynn Cooke, Anders Holm, Marcus Jantti, Kees van Kersbergen, Shelley Lundberg, Luis Medina, Brian Nolan, Adam Przeworski,

Jackie Scott, Michael Shalev, Tim Smeeding, Jane Waldfogel and Chris Whelan. And the DEMOSOC group at Pompeu Fabra has become a great home for my academic life. During the final stages of this book I was given a really welcome breather and chance to concentrate, all thanks to the Institute for Sociology at Copenhagen University and the Danish Institute for Social Research. I would really like to thank Niels Ploug and Carsten Stroeby who made this opportunity possible.

And to underscore the importance of a good childhood, I dedicate this book to

David and Jacob
Barcelona and Copenhagen, Autumn, 2008

Introduction

The past few decades have been marked by turbulent change. Turbulent indeed, since the well-trodden corner stones of society, as described in any standard textbook, are eroding as new principles of social life emerge with a thrust that few would have expected. The 'logic of industrialism' used to be a forceful synthetic concept for what propelled our life as workers, our place within the social hierarchies, and the kind of life course we could expect to follow. As, now, two-thirds of economic activity is centred on servicing, the concept is clearly outmoded. The male breadwinner family is, likewise, becoming an endangered species and what were – only a generation ago – considered 'atypical' families are now the mainstay. Those who take their clues from the media see, mostly with alarm, globalization as a gargantuan force that destroys everything we have come to cherish. Technologies evolve constantly but rarely with the degree of abruptness and with such a comprehensive impact as we have seen over the past decades.

The focal point of this book is a less noticed, but certainly not lesser, fount of revolutionary upheaval, namely the changing status of women. The quiet revolution of women's roles, as Claudia Goldin (2006) calls it, is arguably a close rival to new technologies in terms of its seismic aftershocks touching, directly and indirectly, all major social institutions. And, like its rivals, it has not yet come to full maturation. Incomplete revolutions tend to be associated with major disequilibria.

The social sciences have, for some years now, scrambled to catch the driving logic of the new social order. Too often, our efforts amount to little more than labelling. Following Daniel Bell

I, too, came to embrace the post-industrial thesis. Those who feel closer to the humanities have been more inclined to identify the new world in post-modern terms. And still others see us becoming infused with post-materialism. Few have managed to move beyond pasting a 'post' on the past.

I can think of three reasons why we have so much difficulty grasping the nature of societies that experience major transformations. There is first the sceptical scholar's call for caution: there is no need to dramatize because, most probably, the social world continues as always to adapt and adjust in a gradual and piecemeal fashion. Most of what we see today is basically an extension of what we experienced yesterday. The rising chorus of determined 'post-something' advocates affirms, however, that more radical change is afoot.

The second reason has to do with the increasingly fragmented sociological enterprise. Population ageing occurs very rapidly and is undoubtedly associated with profound alterations in the ways our society and economy function. But those who attack the issue remain by and large narrowly focused on the immediate correlates of ageing, be it the emerging need for elderly care or the bleak prospects for welfare state finances. Disciplinary compartmentalization may, likewise, explain why we have been rather unable to identify how revolutionary indeed is the changing role of women. The issue has been hugely dominated by writers whose analytical lens sees little other than gender inequalities. If we are experiencing the kind of *Great Transformation* that Karl Polanyi (1944) depicted in his grandiose exploration of capitalism's rise, then we need evidence that goes far beyond discrete components of the social order. A great transformation is more likely to be unfolding if there are visible interactions and synergies at work between the many components involved. We need to link it all together.

And the third reason, paradoxically, stems from the fact that those few who do venture into holistic analysis are rather disinclined to offer concise empirical explanation. Linking it all together is an intellectual enterprise that easily can monopolize one's entire academic career and also one that demands an extraordinarily synthetic mind. I think it is fair to say that holistic efforts have, so far, produced frustrating reading. The labellers may furnish suggestive vignettes but they shun away from any systematic attention to the precise causalities that operate. And the macroscopic pulling-it-all-together efforts, such as Manuel Castells's (1996) three volumes on the network society, tend to fall into a functionalist mode. Efforts to join all the pieces of the puzzle together in one great tableau yield, most likely, the uninspiring insight that everything is related to everything. In either case, such scholarly efforts are essentially immune to empirical falsification and this is probably why they have failed to resonate much in the scientific debates.

I am no sociological Michelangelo and will not try my hand at a sociological version of the Sistine Chapel. As the book's title suggests, my aim is to tackle the (unfinished) revolution of women's roles. I am far from the first one to do so. Better and brighter minds have had a go at it for decades. I do see it as an inherently revolutionary process precisely because it has turned upside down so many well-established ways of being and doing. My principal argument, however, is that the so far incomplete nature of the revolution is provoking serious disequilibria in our society. These are particularly evident on three fronts: far fewer children than we desire, way too little investment in the quality of our increasingly few children, and population ageing. A major concern is that the female revolution may also be the harbinger of new inequalities and possibly even of greater social polarization.

Can these disequilibria be adequately managed by families themselves? Can we place our faith in the market? My answer will be: probably not. And this is why the welfare state, yet again, is placed centre stage of my analyses. The colossal feminist literature focuses, like I do, on the need for a new social policy. For the most part it is, however, narrowly concerned with equality issues related to ingrained patriarchy, gender discrimination and the dilemmas of reconciling work and family. I think we all agree that equity is *sine qua non* for a workable remodelling of our society. My analyses aim, however, to also tackle the efficiency issues related to welfare state adaptation. In basic terms, the real challenge I pose myself is to identify a model that is truly optimal in the Paretian sense. This implies, firstly, that any gains in efficiency (say, greater production) cannot be won at the cost of more inequity; vice versa, welfare improvements may be desirable in their own right but they will not produce an optimal outcome if, simultaneously, they jeopardize efficiency. And, secondly, we can say that we have attained a distributive optimum when there is no imaginable alternative allocation which would improve the position of some without worsening that of others.[1] In chapters 3–5, I do my best to adopt these principles in my search for, respectively, a new family policy, a strategy for investing in our children's life chances, and a retirement reform that ensures not only financial sustainability but also greater fairness between and within generations.

I have, with scant success, ventured into political sloganeering in the naive belief that this would help our politicians see the light. My preferred slogan is 'pension reform begins with babies'. It is a useful kind of sound bite because it connects the stages of people's biographies, highlighting how important is early childhood for people's life chances. An approach that adopts a life-course perspective constitutes, I believe, a potentially very powerful tool of analysis. Firstly, it allows, indeed compels, us to link social realities in a non-functional manner. The stages of the life cycle are causally connected, and if we can identify the social mechanisms that link well-being or social problems at one stage, say old age, to conditions in an earlier stage, we are far better equipped to identify the forces that shape the lives of individuals and the fate of social communities. Were we able to persuade our politicians that everything begins with babies, it is very likely that we would see less inequality and greater productivity in the future. Good child policies are likely to result in a truly non-trivial Pareto improvement.

Identifying Revolutionary Change

We can often find historical precedence for what we identify as novel in society. Much attention has been dedicated to the apparent revolution of the family, not least because it is closely associated with rising welfare inequalities. We see income

[1] For an excellent presentation of the Paretian optimum principle, see Rawls (1967).

polarization between dual-earner career couples at the top and single-earner or, worse, workless couples at the bottom.

The conventional nuclear family is increasingly minoritarian, facing stiff competition from a plethora of 'atypical' alternatives such as cohabitation, single-person and lone-parent households. A superficial glance at contemporary behaviour would indeed suggest that the family, as we once knew it, may eventually end up as yet another exhibit in our sociological Jurassic Park. In Scandinavia and North America almost half of all marriages end in divorce, and more and more people appear to shun marriage altogether. If they do marry, it is far later than what used to be the norm. A sizeable group of women, particularly in the US, opts deliberately for lone motherhood. In Scandinavia, almost half of all children are now born outside marriage. And the timing of our decisive life events has undergone distinct changes. We increasingly postpone decisions regarding marriage and births, but we also anticipate others, like retirement. Key life events are, moreover, becoming disconnected. Decisions about motherhood and marriage appear increasingly as uncoupled whereas, once, the twain were basically synonymous. To this we must add the substantial proportion of contemporary women who remain childless or who seem to limit parenthood to one child. A large part of the advanced world appears to have slid into what demographers term a 'lowest-low' fertility syndrome. This syndrome remains quite puzzling to social scientists.

A closer examination of family statistics will reveal a paradoxical panorama. If we choose the post-war decades as our benchmark, we see revolution everywhere. A longer historical scan produces, however, a picture of surprising stability. It turns out, for example, that the US rate of lone motherhood in the 1980s is basically identical to 100 years earlier, and this holds too for the proportion of never-married women and for median age of marriage. The same pattern is evident in Scandinavian fertility behaviour. Mean age at first birth is almost 30 today which is identical to 100 years ago but 5 years later than in 1960.

There are two important points to be drawn from this. One is that we must be careful indeed when we infer revolutionary transformation from data on change. Post-war social scientists, like Gary Becker and Talcott Parsons, erred tremendously in their assumption that the stable nuclear family marked the culmination of an epochal evolution towards modernity. In fact, it is now clear that mid-twentieth-century family behaviour was an historical anomaly in virtually all key dimensions. The jump in fertility that produced the baby-boom generation represented, in historical terms, little more than a brief interlude.

The second point is arguably even more important. If we examine social facts and phenomena, we will probably always encounter historical precedents and conclude accordingly that there is nothing new under the sun. But the social sciences are only relevant when they move beyond commentary on social facts and attempt to identify the underlying driving forces that produce the facts to begin with.

In the case of family formation I doubt that many will be surprised to learn that the primary causes behind lone parenthood or non-marriage are different today from what they were a century ago. In the past, widespread poverty meant that people postponed marriage and parenthood. As I shall discuss in chapter 1, postponement today is primarily driven by women's quest for autonomy. In the past, lone motherhood was very much associated with widowhood; today it is mainly the result of divorce. A century ago, a large share of women remained unmarried and childless because they were condemned to a life of servitude in the homes of the privileged classes. Today, unmarried and childless women tend to be professionals and managers – often the progeny of those same privileged classes.

The family example can easily be generalized. Take the emergence of the service economy, heralded as the cornerstone of post-industrial societies. The share of service employment had already eclipsed manufacturing many decades ago. The pace of service growth has been very rapid over the post-war era and this has of course helped fuel the notion of a revolutionary transformation. Some service industries, like those related to information technologies, are indisputably of very recent origin. But a huge mass of the 'new' service economy jobs are simply the same that once were performed within families and manufacturing firms. Families have externalized a lot of caring, food preparation, laundry, and cleaning; firms have externalized their design, marketing and accountancy departments.

The kinds of national accounts data we use obscure this process of externalization and lead us to believe that we live in an entirely new world. As before, it is perhaps not so much the social facts – in this case servicing – that signal a transformation as the underlying causal mechanisms. A century ago, service consumption was primarily driven by the privileged rich. They were no doubt intensive service consumers, surrounding themselves with an army of maids, nannies and servants – the very same that found it difficult to reconcile servitude with their desires for children and marriage. But aggregate demand for services remained limited because the privileged classes represented a very small consumer group, statistically speaking. In contrast, today's service economy is driven by the broadening of purchasing power throughout the population and, no less importantly, by the disappearance of cheap domestic servants and of the housewife.

All this is not to say that contemporary society exhibits nothing that is historically novel. The past decades have produced extraordinary technological leaps that, in turn, have massive repercussions on earnings, income distributions, and citizens' career prospects. Over the same decades, albeit often with lags, the population has enjoyed a degree of educational and skill upgrading that is historically unprecedented.

The shift from homemaker to a lifetime dedication to employment certainly rivals technology in terms of suddenness and velocity. The momentum has, in this case, been little short of revolutionary. Consider the international forerunners. In Sweden and the US, the rate of female employment hovered around 35% in the 1950s and is now 75% in the former, and 71% in the latter country. The big acceleration started in the 1970s when continuous lifetime employment among mothers became the norm. In laggard countries, such as in Southern Europe, the transformation of women's roles occurs at an astonishing pace. Since 1990 the overall female employment rate in Spain has jumped by 65% and, if we focus on younger women with children, female employment is now close to US rates.

Some have questioned whether this change represents a true 'revolution', arguing that most women in the past were not merely housewives but also active contributors to the family economy, especially in agriculture. Since such work remains unaccounted for in formal statistics we may, like in the example of the service economy, face a spurious kind of change because of inadequate statistical information. Historical data on family work in the farm economy, such as tending to animals or growing vegetables, suggest that the phenomenon was common, but also that it was a minor, if not marginal, activity in terms of time dedication. But as I shall demonstrate, the world of home production has undergone a massive transformation in the past decades. Couples may still 'do gender'; traditional gender norms persist. Yet, there is absolutely no doubt that gender specialization is eroding.

Here is one aspect of the female revolution whose logic certainly does not sit well with Gary Becker's theory of the family. The evidence I shall marshal shows that couples do not decide on the basis of their respective productivities as much as on the basis of power relations and spousal preferences.

The revolution of women's roles coincides with the rise of the knowledge economy. Both are more likely than not to produce new and more intense inequalities – on almost all fronts that matter for social welfare. This is the central theme of chapter 2. Goldin and Katz (2008) argue persuasively that technological change is not inherently inegalitarian. The knowledge economy will primarily produce inequality if human capital fails to match its progress. They attribute the rather dramatic rise in US earnings differentials to the fact that university enrolments have stagnated over the past 30 years. I shall argue that the human capital deficit in advanced nations extends beyond the confines of formal education. Cognitive as well as non-cognitive skills are essential to a knowledge intensive system of production, and these are largely acquired very early on in childhood. The welfare of families is therefore the mainspring of a well-functioning economy. For equity reasons there are no doubt very strong reasons for why we need welfare state reform. Children's opportunities remain far too conditioned on the luck of birth. This certainly implies inequity but also wasted human capital. The central point I intend to follow throughout this book is that by and large efficiency reasons propel us towards reforms designed to enhance equality. The question then boils down to 'what reforms, more precisely'?

In chapter 3, I make a case for a new family policy. Picking up on some of the arguments I made in previous books, the essence of a workable family policy is one that maximizes families' capabilities via 'defamilialization', in particular of caring needs. Perhaps the single most important point is that family policy needs to accelerate the maturation of the female revolution. As long as the latter remains incomplete we shall see the proliferation of inequalities, if not polarizing, tendencies.

In chapter 4, I argue for a social investment strategy on behalf of children. The core issue is that social inheritance continues to exert a powerful effect on children's life chances. Rising social inequalities are bound to worsen this. There are two issues at stake. For one, the persistence of unequal life chances implies that, so far, the modern welfare state has been rather unsuccessful in its promotion of more equality of opportunity. For another, failure to ensure maximum productivity in today's children will endanger their own individual future but also that of society at large. If we desire more economic wealth, we must do something serious about the opportunity structure.

I, like so many, will retire in the decades to come. The quality of my retirement years will depend on the productivity of very small cohorts. And this brings me to chapter 5 whose title would have been an apt slogan for my unsuccessful political campaign. Unlike what has been claimed in most of the debate, the real dilemma of ageing is not so much the possibility of a generational clash. The major challenge lies in forging a reform that addresses the much more important *intragenerational* inequalities that prevail. And as I maintain in chapter 4, these are as much the outgrowth of inequalities in childhood. I should therefore perhaps rephrase my slogan to: 'all good reforms begin with babies.'

The Multi-Equilibrium Society: a Theoretical Framework

Some pages ago I made the claim that ongoing changes in women's roles and in demographic behaviour produce societal disequilibria. This is too vague. It might be more fruitful to think of contemporary societies as constituted of multiple equilibria. In economics, an equilibrium refers to a situation in which the fundamentals of economic behaviour are common knowledge and in which economic agents are certain about each other's behaviour. Sociologists would identify the same in terms of a pervasive, possibly hegemonic, normative order that guides individuals' preferences, behaviour and expectations towards others. Certainly, non-cooperation or deviance can occur in a stable equilibrium. The equilibrium will reproduce itself to the extent that norm-breakers do not succeed in establishing an alternative normative formula towards which a growing number of individuals is attracted. In other words, a stable equilibrium can be identified in terms of its gravitational pull. Medina (2005) uses the concept of 'basin of attraction' to describe the same logic.

The emergence of multiple equilibria occurs, then, when society is composed of several competing 'basins of attraction'; citizens are pulled in different directions, espousing rival preferences and normative standards of conduct. As regards women's roles and family behaviour, the presence of multiple equilibria is not difficult to identify. In the wake of World War II emerged what one might term the *Becker equilibrium*, a convergence towards a modal pattern of gender and family behaviour – so eloquently theorized by Gary Becker (1981). The fundamentals of this equilibrium can be found in any sociological textbook from the 1960s: a nuclear family with the male as breadwinner, and the female as homemaker; early marriage and first births combined with high fertility, stable partnerships and low rates of divorce, singlehood, and childlessness. This is the world of *Ozzie and Harriet*, one of the most popular American TV programmes of the epoch.

The concluding decades of the twentieth century saw the emergence of a rival equilibrium, constructed around a decidedly contrasting set of normative and behavioural fundamentals. It is, above all, identifiable in terms of women's quest for human capital, economic autonomy and lifetime dedication to paid work which, concomitantly, redefines family life. We might accordingly speak of a possible new *gender-equality equilibrium*. As I examine in more detail in this book, we must be very careful about the associated fundamentals. The new normative world does *not* include a renunciation of motherhood; the two-child norm remains basically intact as a preference – albeit not necessarily in terms of behaviour. Indeed, as I argue, the huge gap between desired and realized fertility is one basic characteristic of a third, unstable equilibrium in contemporary societies. In any case, the gender-equality equilibrium represents a different logic in terms of how citizens combine family and economic independence; the move towards a workable, positive-sum formula for reconciling the twain includes a recast welfare state and different ways of 'doing gender', such as the dual-career couple and less role specialization.

As most feminists lament, the gender-equality equilibrium is far from dominant, let alone hegemonic. In fact, it is in the process of being constructed. Were we to take attitudes as a guide, the data that I show in chapter 1 suggest that the Becker equilibrium may continue to describe the life of perhaps a third of Americans or Southern Europeans, but hardly 10% of the Scandinavians. This does not imply that 70% of Americans or 90% of the Swedes have fully embraced the gender-equality equilibrium. All data available suggest that a very large proportion of contemporary citizens find themselves in a third, unstable equilibrium.

An *unstable equilibrium*, as the word suggests, lacks any strong gravitational pull. It represents a basic indeterminacy in terms of guiding people's beliefs and choices, a lack of commonly shared standards identifying 'what is best'. It can be likened to a halfway house, a basin that lacks 'the ability to attract'. An unstable equilibrium is therefore likely to be associated with sub-optimal results; the lack of any good fit between desires and outcomes. The title of this book, *The Incomplete Revolution*, was chosen to stress the double fact that (1) we are historically moving from one equilibrium to another, and therefore find ourselves with an unstable equilibrium that (2), produces sub-optimal outcomes. The latter are visible on many fronts. Very low fertility levels are perhaps the most visible signal of the unstable equilibrium, a point also made by Feyrer et al. (2008). But in the ensuing chapters I argue that the inadequate maturation of the emerging gender-equality equilibrium also produces more income inequality, mainly because the adoption of the dual-career norm is limited to the top end of the social pyramid, and more polarization between families in terms of parenting and child investments.

Much of the feminist literature tends to assume that a truly gender-egalitarian order will render marriage irrelevant. I share Oppenheimer's (1997) scepticism in this regard. I think we can all agree that new family forms are emerging and that formal marriage is but one among several options available in the pursuit of partnership. Since the gender-equality equilibrium remains far from hegemonic and is, indeed, still being constructed, we probably cannot yet fathom what all the fundamentals of the new equilibrium will look like. It is possible that many of the atypical family forms we register in contemporary society represent the unstable equilibrium rather than any future normative order. The fact that divorce and single parenthood are increasingly biased towards the working class and not towards the vanguard of the gender-equality equilibrium suggests this may be the case.

The real analytical challenge is not to identify and classify equilibria, but rather to explain their dynamics and identify their consequences. In the writings of Gary Becker or Talcott Parsons we find little, if any, attention to the historical dynamics that produced the post-war family norm, and even less to the forces that might undo it. They basically took it for granted that the nuclear, male breadwinner model was here to stay. How might we theorize the dynamics of a multi-equilibrium society? There need, in my view, to exist two kinds of drivers: one has to do with a force that alters the core fundamentals of an equilibrium; the other has to do with enabling conditions. The former is likely to be endogenous; the latter exogenous.

What, in the first place, produced the Becker equilibrium? The hegemony of the male-breadwinner nuclear family emerged primarily because a lifelong dedication to housewifery became possible also for working-class women. Why? Primarily because the post-war epoch produced full (male) employment and because huge productivity gains resulted in steadily rising wages, all of which meant that working-class women no longer needed to work in traditional female jobs like textiles and cleaning. The logic is very similar to Krugman's (1991) macroeconomic theory of multi-equilibrium dynamics: shifts in the productivity of factor endowments produced new expectations regarding returns that, in turn, became a self-fulfilling prophecy, accelerating the maturation of industrial capitalism.

The same logic can also be cited for the gradual erosion of the Becker equilibrium and the emergence of a multi-equilibrium state. With rising educational attainment, women became endowed with greater productivity in the market place and, thus, the returns to lifetime employment dedication rose. To a growing proportion of women – and, as a consequence, of men too – female economic autonomy, less gender specialization and a dual-earner based partnership became normative – 'the thing to do'. This transition, however, required exogenous drivers. As is so often stressed, women's autonomy was, in the first round, spurred by birth control technologies, the abolition of marriage banns and the advent of divorce laws (Goldin, 1990). Very similar to Krugman's (1991) model, birth control and divorce created, via their associated externalities, strong diffusion effects that pushed society towards an alternative equilibrium. As divorce rates rose, it became increasingly socially acceptable while simultaneously creating a new and growing marriage market of divorcees. Yet, we now realize that these were necessary but also insufficient preconditions for any gender-equality equilibrium to develop as hegemonic.

The core problem lies in the inherent incompatibilities built into any gender-equality equilibrium. These spring from fundamental changes in individuals' preference sets. Becker's (1981) unitary family utility function may have been credible in a world where normative abidance was truly hegemonic, where few really neither questioned the reigning family model nor could even envisage a more attractive alternative. The changing role of women will almost inevitably undermine this. Firstly, women's quest for autonomy means that spouses are more likely to pursue distinct – and potentially contradictory – preferences. If women desire to maximize their productive potential, they will seek to minimize dedication to tasks that get in its way – such as housework. Secondly, to the extent that women's desire for motherhood has not weakened appreciably – which is what the data suggest – women will automatically face severe problems of reconciling their double preference for children and careers.

This said, the identification of those preconditions that are sine qua non for any gender-equality equilibrium to gain dominant normative status becomes rather evident. One, partnerships need to be founded on alternative normative principles and this means above all new rules for gender specialization. As I examine in more detail in this book, gender equalization in home production is under way. But as so many have stressed, the pace is rather slow and hugely biased in favour of the higher educated. Here we witness one very clear manifestation of an unstable equilibrium, of family practices that remain largely undetermined. If continued gender specialization were simply driven by the spouses' relative market productivities, we would interpret it as abiding by the old Becker equilibrium. The data, however, tell us that spousal productivities offer a poor explanation. Hence, many sociologists simply conclude that couples continue to 'do gender'.

What might trigger a rupture on this front? If rupture implies that men will acquiesce to a gender-egalitarian division of tasks, the answer should lie in either of two triggers: one, as women amass more bargaining power within marriage, they may compel the husband to embrace more equality; two, the choice of partners becomes premised on different logics compared to the past. As I shall describe further on, marital behaviour among the highly educated appears increasingly based on shared preference sets. Hence, assortative mating is on the rise.

The second major precondition for the female revolution to succeed lies in welfare state adaptation. My core assumption is that endogenous drivers are insufficient; that the maturation of a gender-equality equilibrium requires an exogenous input that moves us out of the present unstable equilibrium and its associated sub-optimalities. If we are moving towards a normative standard according to which professional self-realization as well as parenthood is desired similarly across the gender divide, an internal reallocation of home production will, on its own, not suffice to reconcile preferences. Recent contributions to fertility analysis argue persuasively that a return to higher birth rates requires a more gender-egalitarian welfare state (McDonald, 2002). We can generalize this insight. The leading argument I present in this book is that welfare state adaptation is sine qua non if we aim for a stable and hegemonic equilibrium. And as the patient reader will see, much of the evidence that I include in this book serves to underscore the urgency of escaping from the clutches of the unstable equilibrium that, in contemporary societies, dominates our behaviour as partners, parents and workers. I am fully aware of invading upon a sociological territory that has been hugely dominated by feminist writers. I do so because I believe that their often very ideologically based argumentation on behalf of women's causes need not be so. One arrives at pretty much the same kinds of precepts and conclusions from a rational action perspective that aims, simply, to identify superior Pareto outcomes.

Part I The Challenges

1

Families and the Revolution in Women's Roles

Not so many decades ago it was pretty much expected that women, once married, would dedicate their lives to raising children and tending to the home. The shift from housewifery to lifelong employment has been extraordinarily rapid and all-embracing – a seemingly revolutionary transformation (Fuchs, 1988; Goldin, 2006; Esping-Andersen, 2007). Are we really witnessing a revolution? If so, how profound is it? What are its consequences?

Revolution means, literally, a turnaround. Chairman Mao was therefore conceptually correct when he proclaimed that 'revolution is not a dinner party'. A basic definition that probably most would agree upon is the presence of a fundamental transformation of society over a short period of time. Examining long-term trends in female employment, one might interpret the change in women's roles as a long and gradually unfolding process or, alternatively, as an abrupt 'big bang'. Women may now be working but that does not necessarily entail that *society* has been altered in any fundamental way. The really pertinent evidence lies therefore elsewhere, namely whether the way citizens go about their lives has lost any resemblance with past practice.

How might we ascertain this? I suggest that we examine to what extent people's ways of behaving and making decisions are governed by a logic that is distinctly novel; that the rules of the game have, so to speak, been altered. Applied to our concerns, this would entail that women's *and men's* decisions about marriage, parenthood, or work are distinct from that of our forebears (Goldin, 2006). I stress the centrality of men's behaviour for two reasons. One, much of the feminist literature devoted to the subject either ignores men entirely, or it simply assigns them to the status of stalwart patriarchy. Two, a true revolution must produce dialectics.

To ascertain the extent to which the revolution has matured and become encompassing we will therefore need to examine how much it has spread among men and women, and also how deeply it has penetrated all relevant walks of life. For this purpose we need data that convey long-term trends.

Most treatments highlight the centrality of women's economic autonomy. They therefore start – and often end – with trends in educational attainment, paid employment and earnings. This will, however, provide only a very limited understanding. The acid test, in my view, is whether radical change is visible across all the vital dimensions of human life. I shall accordingly also examine partnering, marriage and family formation. Additionally, and perhaps most importantly, we need to know whether, as Hochchild (1989) claims, the revolution was stalled in the domestic sphere. Hence, in the third part of this chapter I turn my attention to couple specialization in child care and housework.

The Masculinization of Women's Life Course

Female education and employment are widely employed to describe the transformation of women's roles. Most studies map the trends over recent decades – for which we have solid data. Since the immediate post-war period saw a significant decline in female employment within the working class we should, as Oppenheimer (1997) warns, select our historical benchmarks with care. If the post-war decades were exceptional in terms of marriage behaviour, childbearing or housewifery, the trends we uncover are likely to be misleading. I therefore begin with a longer snapshot. Table 1.1 draws on historical data for the US, 1900–2000. Together with the Nordic countries, the US can be considered a vanguard in terms of women's new roles. Some might read these data as a long gradual trend towards gender convergence. The sudden acceleration of employment and educational attainment in the final decades of the century suggests, however, the presence of a period-specific shift. The turnaround appears very much centred in the baby-boom generation.

Table 1.1 A century of gender convergence: United States

	Male–female ratio of college degrees	Employment rate: married women	Employment rate: mothers with children, aged 0–6
1900	4.2	6	n.a.
1920	1.9	9	n.a.
1940	1.4	14	11*
1960	1.9	32	19
1980	1.5	50	45
2000	1.1	73	63

Sources: US Census, Historical Statistics. Washington DC: Bureau of the Census (1970) and Statistical Abstracts of the United States (2006)
*1948

Educational attainment can be interpreted as a measure of human capital endowments: that is, of career prospects and earnings potential. In the US, high school completion had already become gender neutral in the post-war years and is, in any case, a poor measure of a person's career potential in the new knowledge economy. I therefore focus, like Goldin (1990), on the male–female ratio in terms of college degrees. We observe a first major leap towards gender parity during the early decades of the twentieth century. This was when upper-class girls began to enter higher education. But after this first leap, we see protracted stability. A second decisive burst arrived in the most recent decades, but this second leap cannot, however, be attributed solely to female inroads in academia. An important part of the story is the stagnation in men's college attainment (Goldin and Katz, 2008).

We are likely to go wrong if we only examine overall female employment levels. This is so because unmarried women have always boasted fairly high participation rates that then dropped sharply subsequent to marriage and childbirth.[1] It therefore seems more appropriate to focus on married women, and on mothers with small children. Both undoubtedly provide a superior measure

[1] The employment rate of single women in the US fluctuated between 40 and 45% over most of the twentieth century, jumping to 60–65% in the last decades (US Census, Historical Statistics, Series D49–62. Washington DC: US Census [1970]).

of equalization (Blossfeld and Hakim, 1997). As we see, married women's labour force attachment grew slowly and steadily up until the 1960s, but then we register a major burst in the latter part of the century. No data on maternal employment exist prior to 1948. In any case, here the pattern is definitely consistent with a non-gradual interpretation of trends.

With some noticeable deviations, the US pattern is quite representative of the experience elsewhere. Female educational attainment now exceeds that of males throughout most of Europe. As to employment, the transformation began a bit earlier in Scandinavia – in the 1960s – and was comparatively both faster and more comprehensive. In Sweden, the participation rate of mothers with small children stood at 38% in the early 1960s, rose to 54% during the ensuing decade, and then skyrocketed to 82% in the 1980s – a level that has been maintained ever since (Hoem, 1995). Britain, however, exhibits a more gradual evolution over the past century. Yet, the fact that married women's employment rate has climaxed at only 60% suggests that the transformation of women's roles remains rather incomplete (Scott, 2008).

These figures exaggerate the revolutionary thrust because, until the 1990s, much of the growth was in part-time work. But over the past decades this has changed as full-time, lifelong employment begins to take hold. The prevalence of part-time commitments may, indeed, serve as a good indicator of where any country finds itself along the revolutionary path. In Britain, Germany and the Netherlands, part-time work is the norm among women with children. In the Nordic countries, the housewife has essentially disappeared and part-time employment, especially in Denmark, is now primarily used as a temporary bridge between maternity leave and the return to a normal work schedule (Blossfeld and Hakim, 1997; Boeri et al., 2005). Economically speaking, the life course of Scandinavian women has definitely become masculinized.[2]

But the incidence of part-time employment is of little relevance in gauging trends in Southern Europe simply because labour

---

[2] In Denmark, the proportion of women who defined themselves as housewives dropped from 43% in 1974 to 3% in 1991; in Sweden, from 26% to 5% (Christoffersen, 1993; Korpi and Stern, 2008).

market regulation has marginalized its existence. More generally, Continental and, especially, Southern Europe exemplify a delayed transformation. In Italy and Spain, maternal employment has only very recently exceeded the 50% barrier. This laggard status may very well be attributed to the absence of part-time opportunities. In any case, these latecomers are now catching up very rapidly (Boeri et al., 2005). In fact, female employment in Spain jumped from 30% in 1995 to 53% in 2007: a 77% leap over a decade! The pace of change is even more visible when we focus on younger women whose participation rate is rapidly approaching 70%. All indications are that the new female cohorts now embrace a lifelong commitment to employment – even despite the lack of part-time jobs and the relatively hostile environment in terms of reconciling work and motherhood (Esping-Andersen, 2007). To illustrate, 42% of Spanish women report that 'working is the most important thing in life', and two-thirds of all women 'would not leave their job if they had children' (Cordon and Sgritta, 2000). A fairly similar (and rapid) catch-up is evident also in Germany and the Netherlands where, however, the predominance of part-time employment suggests that women in these countries are hesitant to embark on a full-fledged revolutionary path.

In any case, the acid test is whether women's new economic status is accompanied by genuinely new behavioural logics. Women's life course choices were traditionally made in a context of economic dependency and major societal constraints. Marriage bans were, for example, not uncommon. As so many writings have argued, the changing role of women has very much been driven by the quest for more autonomy and equality (Fuchs, 1988; Sorensen and McLanahan, 1987; Goldin, 1990; Hakim, 1996). Economic autonomy should, almost by definition, increase with the intensity of female employment in terms of hours worked and, of course, in terms of a lifelong commitment. Traditionally, wives' earnings represented a marginal contribution to family income. To illustrate, in 1960 wives contributed zero income in 61% of American families, whereas now the dual-earner model is the norm. In Scandinavia, wives' earnings now account for, on average, 40–45% of total income. The somewhat lower rate of female employment in the US and elsewhere, especially among less educated women, explains why American wives' contribution is lower (32%), and even lower in countries like Germany, the Netherlands, or Italy (around 25%).[3]

An excellent indicator of 'revolution' would be one that reveals how women make their employment decisions. Traditionally, when wives did work it was primarily as second earners. They worked so as to supplement the husband's earnings or, as Hakim (1996) puts it, to earn 'pin-money'. This implies that women's choices were largely dictated by the partner's earnings. Recent US studies suggest that this logic is in rapid decline. Labour supply, at least among more educated women, is now decided almost exclusively on the basis of own preferences and perceived opportunities. However, less educated women still tend to see themselves as secondary workers (Pencavel, 1998a; Blau et al., 2006; Blau and Kahn, 2007; Lundberg and Pollak, 2007). A recent study highlights the abruptness of this change, showing that the decline of the secondary worker status is highly concentrated among younger women (Kim and Rodriguez-Pueblita, 2005).

Maternity is a key issue in women's work-life choices due to the opportunity costs associated with employment interruptions. Here again the evidence points towards a sharp break with the past. Women in general, and the highly educated especially, take fewer and far shorter maternity breaks. This is brought out very well in Dex et al. (2008), who assemble cohort specific trends in post-first birth interruptions for Britain. Women born in the pre-war epoch typically interrupted for 10–12 years. Those born in the 1940s would interrupt less – 6 years – and from then on we see an abrupt decline to about 1 year. The gap by education is, however, noticeable. The highly educated now return very quickly to work, while the median low-skilled woman will exit for about 4 years. To be sure, the British case is not representative of the world at large. On one hand, there are some countries – most notably Germany – where birth-related interruptions still remain very long among the majority of women (Waldfogel et al., 1999). To this we should, however, add that Germany boasts exceptionally

---

[3] Author's estimations from the European Community Household Panel (last wave) and from the US PSID data.

high rates of childlessness among career women. The Nordic countries, Denmark in particular, represent yet another pattern, one in which the norm is to return immediately after completed maternity leave. In fact, as Waldfogel et al. (1999) argue, mothers are far more likely to resume their careers when offered adequate leave opportunities. In Southern Europe, where leave provisions are ungenerous and brief, we find yet another essentially bi-modal pattern: either they return quickly or they simply exit from the labour market.

A New Logic of Family Formation?

The masculinization of women's economic life should have major repercussions on decisions regarding family and motherhood. In the neo-classical theory of the family, marriage was a vehicle for specialization in home and market production (Becker, 1981). Increased gender convergence in human capital implies that the gains from marriage decline. As partners' market productivities become more similar, the basic rationale for gender specialization in home production should disappear. A very large body of literature has linked falling marriage rates, increased family instability, the emergence of 'atypical' families and also low fertility to women's new roles.

Statistically speaking, the association would seem obvious. Changing marital behaviour seems to coincide with women's increased economic independence (Cherlin, 1992; Fuchs, 1988; McLanahan and Casper, 1995). But when we examine the trends more closely, the direct link between female autonomy and marriage and divorce appears far less obvious. There is, to be sure, a decline in marriage among very dedicated career women, but the phenomenon is far more concentrated among less educated women. The same obtains for divorce and single motherhood. In other words, the break with conventional marital patterns appears especially acute among those women whose employment status has changed the least.

Generally speaking, the old convention of marriage followed by childbearing has been replaced by a proliferation of alternative biographical paths, including cohabitation and births outside wedlock

(Rindfuss, 1991). The spread of cohabitation seems to confirm the idea that marriage has lost its appeal. Cohabitation is now standard practice in Scandinavia and France, representing a third of all households. It is also gaining ground rapidly in most other advanced nations. What is more, cohabitation is increasingly a stable, long-time arrangement. And opinion data demonstrate that the majority of citizens regard it as basically equivalent to family (Kiernan, 2004; Ghysels, 2004). Being married and having children have ceased to be virtually synonymous. We should, nonetheless, be wary of strong generalizations since the meaning of cohabitation clearly varies across countries. In some cases, cohabitation looks more like a prelude to, or a testing-ground for, marriage; in others, most clearly in Scandinavia, cohabitation is now de facto the same as marriage. This difference emerges clearly in fertility behaviour. In Denmark and Sweden about half of all births occur among cohabiting couples; in the rest of Europe, the vast majority of births are found in marital unions (Kiernan, 2004).

Births outside marriage have experienced a quantum leap. In Northern Europe and North America, they represented roughly 10 per cent of all births in 1970. In Scandinavia now, just about half of all children are born to unmarried, but usually cohabiting, parents. Starting from much lower levels, out-of-wedlock births have more than doubled in virtually all countries (Kiernan, 2004: Figure 3.3). Such statistics may, however, distort reality since they combine births in unmarried unions with non-partnered births. Moreover, in some countries, particularly the UK and the US, teenage mothers account for a substantial – but now declining – share of the total. But even in the latter case, the statistics may very well capture a changing logic of decision-making. As several studies emphasize, the decision among young American mothers, in particularly black and less educated women, to raise children alone is motivated by a desire to maintain control of their own and their children's lives (Ellwood and Jencks, 2004).

The spread of divorce is also frequently cited as evidence in favour of the erosion of the family. The divorce rate began to rise sharply in the Nordic countries during the 1960s; in most other advanced countries, one or two decades later. The timing of the take-off will depend, of course, on legislative liberalization. In one group of countries, including Scandinavia and the US, roughly half of all marriages now end in divorce. Elsewhere, with the exception of the Mediterranean countries, the divorce rate now hovers between 35 and 40 per cent. But the Catholic Southern European countries, starting from a base close to zero, have experienced a doubling since the 1980s (Council of Europe, 2001). Stevenson and Wolfers (2006) highlight the generational shift that underpins the surge: divorce rates among Americans, married after 1980, are twice as high as for those who married in the 1950s.

Still, as Oppenheimer (1997) warns, marital instability and cohabitation do not necessarily imply that marriage has become obsolete. The proportion of never-married women may have risen, but the trend is not especially dramatic. Moreover, a large share of cohabiting couples opts eventually for marriage. Behind Oppenheimer's warning is the argument that comparisons with the post-war decades distort our understanding of long-term changes in family life. The problem lies in the fact that, demographically speaking, the post-war era was a short-lived and unique historical parenthesis.

In fact, we see striking parallels between families today and a century ago. In the late 1800s, the average age of marriage was high and the share of lone mothers, never-wed and childless women was substantial, just like now. The post-World War II decades were historically atypical in all respects related to family formation: people suddenly began to marry and have (more) children at younger ages. The proportion of never-married women dropped to a historical low of 14 per cent in 1960, and partnerships were unusually stable (Oppenheimer, 1997: 433). This is also when the male breadwinner family became effectively the norm throughout society.

It is important to recognize, nonetheless, that these cross-century similarities disguise the presence of very different causes. In the distant past a fair proportion of women were domestic servants and nannies and were therefore prevented from marrying and having children. Their lack of economic independence was near-total. Similarly, single motherhood in the nineteenth century was frequently caused by death or disappearance of the father. The typical causes today are found in divorce or, as noted, in the deliberate decision to have children outside a union. What has changed is not so much the desire for marriage or children, but rather the way the decisions are made.

What demographers call the postponement syndrome describes very well the new dynamics of family formation. The average age of marriage and the onset of motherhood have risen sharply over the past decades and, hence, present a striking similarity to nineteenth-century conditions. Postponement reflects, in part, the advent of new constraints, such as longer education, high levels of youth unemployment, or difficulties in accessing the housing market. And, in part, it reflects the emergence of new ways of making decisions. Fertility offers an excellent example. It might be tempting to conclude that the radical drop in fertility signals a weakened desire for motherhood. But this would be a mistake since all available evidence suggests that women throughout the advanced countries continue to adhere to a two-child preference (Kohler et al., 2002; Esping-Andersen, 2002; Sleebos, 2003). Like in the case of matrimony, the desire for children has not changed. What has changed is the way prospective parents decide.

The classical theory of fertility was premised on the assumption that women were economically dependent. It therefore argued that the male's earnings status was a prime predictor of when and if couples decided to have children (Hotz et al., 1997). Most recent studies conclude that the husband's earnings now have little relevance for motherhood. The timing of fertility as well as decisions regarding the number of children seem now primarily related to women's own characteristics, such as career progress, earnings, and job characteristics, and to the presence of family-friendly welfare state policy (McDonald, 2002; Brodmann et al., 2007; Sleebos, 2003; Stier et al., 2001). Job insecurity, unemployment, and reconciliation difficulties are the chief explanations of contemporary low fertility rates throughout most of the advanced countries (Kohler et al., 2002). Mothers' ability to persuade fathers to contribute more to domestic tasks and child care has also been found to influence fertility positively, especially among career women (Brodmann et al., 2007; DeLaat and Sevilla Sanz, 2006; Cooke, forthcoming). Men may therefore have to join the revolution if they want to be fathers.

All this lends support to McDonald's (2000, 2002) argument that the persistence of gender inequalities is probably the single best explanation of low fertility. If that were so, we would expect fertility to be positively related to a society's degree of gender equality. In fact, all available evidence favours such an interpretation. Fertility levels are now positively correlated with the rate of female employment while, three decades ago, the sign was strongly negative (Ahn and Mira, 2002). We see the same tendency as regards education. The historically negative association between women's educational attainment and fertility is now turning positive in the Nordic countries (Esping-Andersen, 2002; Kravdal and Rindfuss, 2008).

Decisions regarding whether and whom to marry have clearly also changed. As already noted, women who face an unattractive marriage market are likely to shun marriage – but not children – altogether. The deteriorating economic position of low-skilled males combined, at least in the US, with high delinquency and incarceration rates among young black and low-educated males, implies a shortage of marriageable men (Wood, 1995). We simultaneously see a marked increase in assortative marriage. Partnerships are increasingly homogamous in terms of education and, almost certainly, of preferences and tastes. This is especially pronounced among the highly educated (Blossfeld and Timm, 2003; Schwartz and Mare, 2005).

If the choice of partner is driven by similarities of human capital, the upshot is that the gains to marriage do not lie in gender specialization, but rather in the opposite. Research has cited a number of alternative logics behind homogamy. One is the prospect of maximizing joint income and thus consumption potential; another lies in the social capital dividend that can be reaped, not only from the spouses themselves, but also indirectly from their parents and social circles; a third has to do with the importance attached to sharing similar values and preferences (Bernardi, 1999; Blossfeld and Timm, 2003; Oppenheimer, 1997; Schwartz and Mare, 2005).

The classical theories of the family in both economics (Becker, 1981) and in sociology (Parsons and Bales, 1955) assumed that the post-war housewife-cum-male breadwinner family signalled the maturation of a long process of modernization. It did not, of course. In fact, if we really wish to come to grips with the nature of women's revolution, we need first to get the story of the housewife right.

The full-time homemaker role was, until World War II, very much a luxury afforded by the more privileged social strata – those who incidentally had the means to hire nannies and domestic servants. A number of factors came together in the postwar decades that allowed working-class families to emulate this model – albeit without the aid of nannies and servants (Esping-Andersen, 1999). One, male workers suddenly experienced a sharp and steady increase in earnings – and a concomitant fall in the risk of unemployment. As Goldin (1990) shows, the rise in female employment prior to the war was primarily concentrated among working-class women. Consistent with traditional behaviour, wives' increased labour supply in the 1930s compensated for the weakened earnings power of males. But once the opportunity arose, working-class women undoubtedly welcomed the housewife option. They were concentrated in low-paid jobs in cleaning, textiles and the clothing industry. The historical irony is that, just as the working class embraced housewifery, the upper middle-class women began to embark on careers. These relatively highly educated women were the pioneers of what we now label the revolution of women's roles. The momentum of the revolution depended, however, on how deeply it came to penetrate down the educational ladder, an issue that I shall address further ahead.

Gender Specialization and Home Production

The data on work histories and family choices may support the notion of revolutionary change. But the case is seriously weakened if, as Hochchild (1989) affirms, it has been stalled in the domestic sphere. Here we should firstly recognize that her evidence was based on the status quo in the 1980s. We have already seen that the real revolutionary momentum began exactly in this period. Additionally, we know from a huge number of time-use based studies that a major redistribution of domestic tasks has occurred over the past two decades. Women have cut down on housework;

men's contribution has increased, admittedly at a slower rate (Bianchi et al., 2000, 2006).

Grunow et al. (2008) provide some evidence that supports the Hochchild hypothesis. Theirs is a rare example of longitudinal analysis, following couples over several years. Their principal finding is that partners typically display gender egalitarian behaviour prior to marriage and childbirth but revert to traditional specialization once the first child is born. And once established, the new and less egalitarian regime becomes permanent. In other words, their findings agree with the dominant view of feminists that conventional gender norms in the domestic sphere are extraordinarily resistant to change, regardless of major upheavals in role patterns throughout society. Unfortunately, it is not clear how far we can generalize their findings. They are based on a small number of observations and on rather crude time-use measures. Moreover, the study was undertaken in a German city and we know that Germans in many respects continue to adhere to traditional gender behaviour to a far larger extent than elsewhere.

Taking one step back we need first to settle one basic question, namely which are the key factors involved in couple specialization in home and market production? The contemporary debate is essentially a debate with Gary Becker's (1981) neo-classical theory of the family.

In the writings of Gary Becker, the male-breadwinner family represents the most efficient arrangement in the pursuit of family welfare. Marriage itself is motivated by exactly these concerns. Becker's (1981) theory of specialization posits that couples will decide purely rationally on who secures income and who tends to the home. Rational choice would imply the absence of normative pressures, sentiments, or ideology. If they aim to maximize joint welfare, the partners will make the decisions based on their respective productivities. The theory assumes a unitary utility function. This implies an assumption of perfectly shared preferences or, alternatively, that family decisions are made by a benign and altruistic dictator who acts on behalf of the whole family's welfare.

This perspective may have seemed uncontroversial in the post-war decades. Since men generally had more education and better earnings prospects, female specialization in domestic tasks would have seemed obvious. Here we should also remember that traditional home production was far more labour intensive and that families had many children. Gender specialization should, at least in theory, decline in tandem with the convergence in gender productivities. As women's educational attainment, earnings and work-life biographies come to resemble men's, the foundations of a gendered division of work should erode. This is, to be sure, perfectly consistent with Becker's theory. And when we add to this the phenomenal progress in household technologies and also the decline in fertility, the unavoidable burdens of home production are eased considerably. To exemplify, washing a load of clothes by hand takes roughly four hours. With a washing machine, the task is reduced to 40 minutes (Ramey, 2006).

Becker's (1981) theory has been criticized for its naivety because of its underlying assumptions and omissions. The assumption of a unitary utility function has been widely questioned, in particular in lieu of women's enhanced autonomy and potential bargaining power. Those familiar with the realities of marriage are, a priori, unlikely to view it as a faithful depiction of their lives. The fact that divorce has become so commonplace suggests that fundamental disagreements are intrinsic to modern marriage. If we add to this the intense reconciliation dilemmas that accompany mothers' dedication to employment, one would expect that conflicts over domestic work burdens should become commonplace – in particular over the undesirable, labour-intensive activities. Many also criticize Becker's model because it ignores the weight of norms, not to mention love, in marital behaviour. Since the theory is couched in a rational choice framework, it assumes that decisions on specialization derive primarily from an assessment of the partners' relative productivities. The latter can be captured by comparing the spouses' respective earnings or, better, wage rates. Empirical research has found only very mixed support for the idea that spouses allocate tasks exclusively on the basis of efficiency maximization. Yet, this does not necessarily imply that they act irrationally, only that they may adhere to alternative kinds of rational calculus.

For both empirical and theoretical reasons, research has come to embrace a number of alternative explanations of specialization, stressing either the importance of bargaining power, time availability, or the persistence of conventional gendered norms. A few have, additionally, emphasized the salience of the institutional environment and, in particular, the welfare state as a vehicle for gender equalization in home production (Fuwa, 2004; Geist, 2005).[4]

The bargaining perspective has been most closely associated with economics, but has also found its way into sociological research. In the former case, this implies the recognition that spouses have individually distinct preference sets and will seek to maximize these by implicitly invoking a threat point. We can think of this as an exit, voice, or loyalty scenario (Gershuny et al., 2005). Loyalty would come closest to the unitary utility framework: no one questions the wisdom of any given arrangement. Voice represents disagreement and hence the need to bargain over rival preferences. And exit is captured by the activation of one's threat point: if the partner is unwilling to budge, negotiations will come to a halt, possibly producing a separation.

To be able to invoke a credible threat, a partner must command outside resources, i.e., resources that do not depend on the partnership itself (Chiappori, 1988). The reasoning here is that a threat, say of divorce, is not convincing if the negotiator is unable to secure for him- or herself an adequate post-divorce living standard. Note here that the threat point need not be exclusively monetary. Lundberg (2005) argues that the presence of a son provides mothers with added bargaining power due to gendered child preferences among fathers. There is some evidence to back up this claim. Lundberg and Rose (2003) show that the risk of divorce declines when at least one child is a boy. To capture family decision-making, economists have applied both cooperative and non-cooperative bargaining models. Most, however, adopt the former, assuming that the partners prefer to reach a common win–win outcome (Browning et al., 1994; Chiappori, 1988, 1992; Pollak, 2005).

Although less formalized, sociological work focuses on the relative command of resources in a broader sense, emphasizing the

---

[4] These different perspectives are reviewed and discussed in Shelton and John (1996).

importance of wives' educational level, income and their degree of economic dependency on the partner (Brines, 1994; England and Budig, 1998; Bianchi et al., 2000; Evertsson and Nermo, 2004). Empirical work in this tradition usually demonstrates that more equality of resources fuels more equality in housework (Bianchi et al., 2000). Yet, the data also suggest that couples are more likely to revert to conventional gendered behaviour when the husband is clearly inferior in terms of his income share or his employment status (Bittman et al., 2003; Brines, 1994; Evertsson and Nermo, 2004; Breen and Cooke, 2005). Similarly, Gupta (1999) compared people before and after partnering and found that marriage produces a decline in men's and an increase in women's housework. Many therefore conclude that traditional gender norms and expectations continue to exert a major influence on how couples specialize.[5]

A large feminist literature has argued that the continued weight of social norms leads couples to re-enact and reproduce conventional gender role patterns. Theoretically speaking, the argument amounts to a frontal attack on Becker's (1981) failure to consider the decisiveness of social norms; empirically, it seeks to offer an explanation for the failure of real progress of gender equality in the home (Berk, 1985), or the process of lagged adaptation, as Gershuny et al. (1994) have termed it.

As I shall show further on, attitude surveys reveal that conventional gender norms do persist. And from the studies cited above we do have abundant evidence that 'doing gender' is pervasive within contemporary families. But as a general theory it probably comes short. All the evidence suggests that a genuine process of equalization is under way, albeit primarily among higher educated couples (Bianchi et al., 2000; Bonke and Esping-Andersen, 2008). Bianchi et al. (2000) find only little support for the 'doing-gender' thesis, but do show that men's contribution to housework increases very little. The main source of gender equalization comes from women's sharp reduction in home production. In any

5   A persuasive argument has been made in favour of the importance of women's *absolute* rather than relative income position. The basic point is that a relative measure does not really inform us about women's real threat point.

case, the dualities of the female revolution seem to be very much in evidence also behind the four walls of the family home. Put differently, we are examining a glass that, to some, is half empty and, to others, half full.

There are other reasons why the 'doing-gender' thesis may lack general validity. It is very likely that there exist social selection processes that we cannot observe behind those couples where husbands' inferior status produces conventional partner specialization. Iyigun (2005), for example, argues that the way that (future) spouses sorted themselves within marriage markets determines how they later end up specializing. There is, in fact, some evidence that a gender-asymmetric division of labour raises the risk of divorce – a clear case of 'exit' (Cooke, 2006). If so, we would expect that inegalitarian, 'doing-gender' arrangements are likely to become ever scarcer.

There is, finally, a tradition that has emphasized the importance of time constraints in the allocation of domestic work (England and Farkas, 1986). Similar to Becker, it is assumed that partners allocate time based on considerations about what would be most rational for family welfare. Time availability is a function of external constraints, mainly market work, and of internal ones, in particular the number and age of children. There is substantial evidence that outside employment leads to less female housework – and that children provoke the opposite. We also know that external time constraints affect women's, but rarely men's, housework contribution. Yet, as Bonke and Esping-Andersen (2008) show, outside employment even on a full-time basis does not produce any reduction in women's time with their children. And, as Bianchi et al. (2000) conclude, overall the evidence for the time availability thesis is rather slim.

Trends and Variation in Couple Specialization

The historical evolution of couple specialization is difficult to reconstruct since we only have reliable and detailed time-use surveys from the 1960s onwards. We do have ethnographic time-use studies that date back about 100 years, usually based on 'typical' worker – or sometimes farming – families (Gershuny,

2000; Ramey, 2006; Esping-Andersen, 1999). Using the typical working-class family as our benchmark, an early American study (done in Indianapolis around 1900) finds that the wife committed 80 weekly hours to home production (and zero hours to market work). The husband spent 66 hours at the job and contributed virtually no hours to domestic work. These are probably reliable estimates considering that a similar kind of study, in this case conducted in Milan, conveys very similar patterns of time use (Esping-Andersen, 1999). Gershuny and Robinson (1988) and Bianchi et al. (2000) have attempted to reconstruct the historical evolution of the household division of labour. They find, by and large, a stable pattern until the 1980s whereafter we register a clear fall in women's relative and absolute contribution and also some increase in men's, particularly with regard to child care. According to Bianchi et al.'s data, men in the 1970s contributed only a third as much as women to housework. But by 1995 their share had risen to a bit more than 50 per cent. Even if women clearly continue to dominate cooking and cleaning, the domestic revolution did not stall completely. Ramey (2006) provides a fairly comparable time series for housework which is, of course, only one part of total home production (see Table 1.2).

These figures tell only part of the story, especially because they exclude child care which just so happens to be an activity where the male contribution has increased very markedly. Since 1985, father's contribution to child care has doubled in the US and elsewhere (Bianchi et al., 2006; Hook, 2006; Bonke and Esping-Andersen, 2008). When we include childcare time, men's domestic hours were 14 per week in 1965, 18 in 1985, jumping to 23 hours in 2000. How do we interpret these data?

The slow historical progress towards gender symmetry seems very much consistent with the 'doing-gender' thesis. It is certainly clear that full-time housewives have experienced very little change over the century, but from the 1980s onwards this is an increasingly small – and probably select – group. But if we compare men with working women, the time-use data do seem to line up well with our earlier portrait of the female revolution, in particular when we add child care to housework hours. In this case, the wife–husband home production ratio was 2.7 in

Table 1.2 A century of gender specialization in the US: average hours of housework per week

	Husbands	Wives, not working	Wives, working
1900	3	60	n.a.
1920	3	56	n.a.
1940	5	55	24
1965	11	55	28
1985	15	45	25
2003	16	45	25

Source: Ramey (2006: Figures 9 and 10)

1965, the earliest year for which we have detailed childcare data. By 1985, the ratio drops to 1.8, reaching 1.6 in 2003.[6] We can illustrate the same point by calculating how much of total home production has been redistributed from women to men. Between 1965 and 2003, women's *total* domestic work declined by 11 hours while men's increased by 4 (Aguiar and Hurst, 2006). Over the period, the total workload fell by about 5 hours. If we were to assign these savings entirely to the woman, we arrive at a net hours' redistribution equivalent to 38 per cent. Couples may still be 'doing gender' but they certainly are doing it much less. And considering the speed of change, I would interpret this as a burst of equalization.

It is well worth exploring gender specialization in more detail, in particular if our aim is to understand whether, and precisely how, women's changing roles affect behaviour and decision-making. Although some gender equalization has undoubtedly occurred, it would also appear far less thoroughgoing than one might expect considering the turnaround in women's roles.

Viewed over time, the gender shift in family duties began in earnest much later than the onset of women's role change. It is not

[6] These data refer to the United States. The trend would look very similar for the Nordic countries. Given the leap in men's childcare dedication in the last decade, one would have expected a more pronounced fall in the gender ratio by 2000. The principal reason why it fails to decline more is the surprising (4-hour) increase in mothers' contribution to child care (see especially Bianchi et al., 2006). The same phenomenon is present in Scandinavia (Bonke and Esping-Andersen, 2008).

really until after the 1980s that we register any serious change, be it in the US or in the Nordic countries. Moreover, the increase in men's effort does not look especially dramatic. The most recent time-use data (from the first decade of the new century) certainly support the half-full glass analogy. Most studies concur that the gap between men and women remains far greater than one would expect on the basis of measurable productivity differentials. Yet, the data also affirm that we are now undergoing a rather significant process of equalization. Table 1.3 shows the changing role of men in housework during the past two decades. The US, to be sure, displays a picture of stagnation – one which has led many to believe that equalization has come to a halt. The Danish data, however, suggest that men and women are moving towards a fair degree of parity. The Spanish trend is especially noteworthy: a 50 per cent leap over only one decade. As Hook (2006) shows, similar equalizing trends are under way in most advanced nations.

Empirical research has mainly focused on paid work or on household chores. The latter represent unpleasant activities (albeit desirable outcomes) that most people would crave to minimize.[7] Housework is, moreover, time-consuming and highlights therefore the dilemmas of reconciling employment and family. In other words, this is where we should expect that spouses' preferences clash. Most studies conclude, however, that inequalities of housework have much less to do with women's bargaining power than with the persistence of conventional gender attitudes (Alvarez and Miles, 2003; Cooke, 2006; Evertsson and Nermo, 2004). This is additionally confirmed by studies of couples where the woman's economic role appears dominant (Brines, 1994). A somewhat different conclusion emerges in studies that examine the interplay of activities. Bianchi et al. (2006) demonstrate that mothers' strong prioritization of children leads them to cut down on housework (and market work) in order to increase their time with the children.

---

[7] Following Juster and Stafford (1985), some time-use surveys include information on the degree of enjoyment obtained from various activities, including housework, paid employment, leisure and child care. Housework systematically scores very low (although making dinner scores rather similar to watching TV).

Table 1.3 Gender equalization of housework: men's share as a percentage of total housework time in couples

	1980s	Twenty-first Century
Denmark	31	41
Spain	23	32
US	32	33

Sources: Danish Time-Use Surveys for 1987 and 2001; the Spanish WSTUS survey for 1991 and for 2003; US data derives from Bianchi et al. (2006: Tables 5A1 and 5A2)

Research on childcare time is surprisingly scarce, perhaps because of the ambiguities involved. Child care can be regarded as parental investment in child quality (Becker and Lewis, 1973), but also as an enjoyable activity in its own right, i.e., a *process benefit* that is independent of any outcome of the self-same activity (Juster and Stafford, 1985; Hallberg and Klevmarken, 2003). Both US and Swedish surveys demonstrate that child-related activities score highest (next to sex) on a 1–10 rank of perceived enjoyment for men and women alike – higher even than most leisure activities. But child care includes also less welcome tasks such as changing diapers. Playing with the children is by far the most popular male activity; being in charge of the children is even more enjoyable to women (Hallberg and Klevmarken, 2003: Table 3).

The logic of preferences with regard to housework and child care should therefore be very distinct within any bargaining and specialization framework. If we ignore for the moment the salience of spousal productivities, we would expect that partners bargain to diminish housework so that they can devote more time to desirable or remunerative activities. Bargaining with regard to child care is more difficult to predict to the extent that it is viewed as a positive activity. It would be useful, then, to distinguish routine from developmental, or active, caring. In the former case, one would expect outcomes similar to those related to housework. In the latter case, one would expect that parents seek to diminish the burden of less desirable activities so as to maximize time with children. If Lundberg's (2005) 'boy-thesis' is correct, mothers' bargaining power should therefore lead to an increase in fathers' contribution to routine care.

Empirical studies focusing on child care are very rare. Hallberg and Klevmarken (2003), Bloemen and Stancanelli (2008) and also Bonke and Esping-Andersen (2008) examine how market work affects childcare time, concluding essentially that, for mothers, higher earnings are not associated with less childcare time. This underscores Bianchi et al.'s (2006) argument that mothers' prioritization of children has intensified. Bonke and Esping-Andersen (2008) find some support for the 'boy-thesis', but only for low-educated fathers. They also find that marital homogamy among the highly educated is especially conducive to egalitarian childcare arrangements. Low-educated homogamous couples behave, however, according to traditional gendered stereotypes.

Empirical studies routinely identify large differences between low- and high-educated couples. Men's contribution to home production is far greater – and has risen more steeply – among the highly educated. Similarly, maternal dedication to children is significantly stronger – and rising – among the highly educated (Bianchi et al., 2000, 2006; McLanahan, 2004). Explaining such stratified patterns is not straightforward. On one hand, it is likely that low-educated women command fewer resources with which to bargain effectively. They tend to have more children, command low earnings and are typically less dedicated to careers. But these factors just beg the question of why, in the first place, such women behave more traditionally. It may be that their higher fertility rates and lower labour supply reflect their stronger identification with conventional family roles to begin with. Shalev (2008) identifies such polarities in behaviour as an expression of distinct social class differences.

And this brings us to the third and, as yet, rather undeveloped dimension of specialization, namely how to distinguish the role of preferences from the effect of productivities. Under what conditions would we expect divergent or unitary preferences?

Common sense would lead us to believe that partners who share a similar social background, culture and education will also display more similar tastes and values. Homogamous couples should, all told, have more identical preferences. But, and herein lies the ambiguity, such couples are also likely to exhibit similar productivities. Among such couples, the returns to gender specialization should approach zero.

The behaviour of homogamous couples is therefore fraught with ambiguity because any observed division of labour may reflect shared preferences or similar productivities. If shared preferences prevail, we would, all told, expect that couples' decision-making should approximate Becker's unitary utility model and, hence, the role of bargaining should be rather limited. If, on the other hand, homogamy only reflects similar productivities, we would expect that bargaining will have important effects on the domestic division of labour, especially since the time-opportunity costs are similar for both partners.

The role of assortative mating has received almost no attention in the empirical literature. One minor exception is research on couples' employment decisions (Pencavel, 1998a). In their study of housework allocation, Evertsson and Nermo (2007) also analysed the impact of homogamy and found that it stimulates more gender equality among the highly educated, but not in low-educated couples. As we shall see below, this is exactly what I also find.

There are several reasons why the prevailing 'doing-gender' thesis might be affected by taking homogamy into consideration. Firstly, the choice sets that lie behind homogamous marriages are likely very different across the educational spectrum. To the extent that higher education constitutes an important marriage market, it also becomes a strong social filter in terms of social background, world outlooks and tastes. And partnering among the highly educated is probably driven more by a lifetime commitment to dual careers. Homogamy at the bottom is most likely the by-product of a wholly different selection process that occurs in very different marriage markets. One would additionally expect that low-educated men and women exhibit more traditional gender norms. We know, for example, that low-skilled women are more likely to adopt the homemaker role and, in most countries, their labour force attachment is relatively weak. Yet, to the extent that homogamous 'low-end' couples also exhibit rather similar productivities, at least in market work, we would expect that bargaining power should matter. Put differently, variations in household specialization may be driven by how education and assortative marriage combine.

We need to develop a methodology that permits us to distinguish empirically between the effect of preferences and of productivities. The task-enjoyment approach developed by Juster and Stafford (1985) offers one potential approach. The problem, though, is that men and women differ very little in how they rank the pleasure of activities. A focus on educationally homogamous couples offers an alternative, and potentially promising, avenue. But we face major obstacles. Firstly, we know that formal education is a very incomplete measure of human capital.[8] Secondly, similar levels of education do not entail similar earnings potential. The earnings power of two PhDs, one in art history, the other in aeronautics, is bound to diverge by a factor of two or three. Thirdly, the gender wage gap varies by education levels and this will also affect the relative productivities (and bargaining power) of spouses across the educational spectrum. To identify relative productivities we therefore also need to measure the spouses' respective wage rates. This, however, poses serious problems of identification since this is exactly the same information that is required in order to construct an optimal bargaining power variable.

To the extent that we can identify convergent productivities, how can we then distinguish their impact from a preference effect? In the following, I adopt two solutions. The first is to construct a measure of productivities that does not correlate with bargaining power. The latter is best measured as the wife's wage rate relative to the husband's, i.e. as a ratio (Pollak, 2005). The greater her relative earnings power, the more she is likely to be economically autonomous. But we need the same wage rate differences to identify productivity differentials. In the analyses that follow, I solve the problem by devising a measure of 'wage rate homogamy', a categorical variable that identifies whether the two partners belong within the same wage rate quartile.

The second solution, one that seems to have never been adopted in empirical research, is to focus on joint time allocation. There are good reasons why this has not been examined since it is only very recently that we have time-use surveys that collect individual time diary data for both members of the same couple. For a number of

---

[8] This will be discussed in greater detail in chapter 4.

countries we now have such data. Data on joint time dedication allows us to distinguish productivities from preferences. If spousal time allocation is primarily based on productivity differentials, the rational decision would be to minimize overlap via substitution strategies. This should especially be the case for the production of positive goods, such as preparing meals or caring for children. But if their time allocation is driven primarily by congruent preferences, the spouses would more likely desire to engage in activities jointly. If preferences reign, the couple would arguably be willing to forego some efficiency. Here, again, this should especially be the case for process benefit activities, such as child care.

In the analyses that follow, I focus on couple specialization in housework and child care. I exploit the most recent (2003) Spanish time-use survey for three reasons. First and foremost it is one of the few existing surveys that permit us to link the time use of both members of the couple – and thus to examine how much they do things together. Secondly, it is a high-quality survey with a large sample size which, then, permits more robust estimation. Time-use studies typically suffer from having too few observations. But most importantly, Spain constitutes a particularly interesting test-case for the 'doing-gender' thesis considering its unusually harsh environment in terms of reconciling careers and family obligations. Previous studies, based on older time-use data, have in fact concluded that couple behaviour in Spain continues to be firmly entrenched in traditional gender patterns (Alvarez and Miles, 2003). For comparison I shall draw on evidence from Denmark which, no doubt, stands as an international vanguard in terms of gender equalization.

If we simply compare averages, there is little doubt that gender inequalities remain substantial in Spain, certainly when compared with Denmark or the US. The female–male housework ratio is 3.1 for Spain (in 2003) compared to Denmark's 1.4 and a US ratio of 2.0.[9]

This pattern extends also to paid work where, in Spain, men dedicate on average four times more hours than women which is

---

[9] Estimated from the 2001 Danish Time-Use Survey and the 2003 Spanish Survey. US data derive from Bianchi et al. (2006: Tables 5A1 and 5A2).

a huge gap when compared to Denmark or the US (in both cases approximately 1.3 times as much).[10]

Our primary aim, though, is to identify change in the logic of family behaviour. This means that we need to disentangle the relative importance of preferences, productivities and bargaining power in the allocation of unpaid work. Although everybody acknowledges the key importance of preferences, these are hardly ever identified. Most studies simply assume their existence. In the analyses that follow I attempt to capture them by constructing a categorical variable of educational homogamy. Since the correlation between education and wages is quite modest (0.4), we can to an extent assume that education captures something else than the productivities associated with human capital. Since I believe that homogamy means something very different in high-education couples compared to the less educated, I also include an interaction term: being homogamous *and* highly educated at once. The variable that captures the degree to which productivities are similar is, again, a dummy based on wage quartiles. If both spouses fall in the same wage quartile, they are categorized as 'similar' with regard to labour market productivity. And to identify the impact of spousal bargaining power, I follow Pollak's (2005) recommendation: the wife's wage rate divided by the combined wage rate of the wife and the husband. It is important that we use wage rates since these are not affected by how much a person happens to work in any given week or month. This variable should therefore capture a person's earnings *potential*.

All the analyses that follow include the standard repertoire of controls: education levels (low, medium and high which correspond to lower secondary, higher secondary and tertiary level). Less than lower secondary is our reference group. I also include controls for weekly work hours outside the home, working in the public sector, having children (also pre-school age children) and three variables that tap whether the couple has the benefit of external help (from family members, most likely grandparents, paid household help and outside child care).

---

[10] The large gap in market work is of course very much driven by the presence of many women with zero paid hours.

As we shall see, education is positively related to more gender equality – which is what all studies find. And, unsurprisingly, we find that child care and, to an extent also housework, is positively associated with the number of children and, in particular, with the presence of small children. Outside help produces interesting gender effects: it clearly helps mothers on the domestic front, especially with regard to housework, but it simultaneously boosts fathers' time with their children. In separate analyses (not shown), I find that help from relatives increases paternal care by 24%. If the child attends day care, the boost to paternal care is 39%. Outside help has, however, no discernible effect on men's contribution to housework.[11]

I estimate regressions separately for husbands and wives, and include also estimates for the proportion of time in the activity that they do jointly – the latter attempting to capture the importance of preferences.[12] I examine solely weekday activities since this is when trade-offs and opportunity costs are most severe (see Tables 1.4 and 1.5).

Table 1.4 tells us that women dedicate more than three times as many minutes as men to housework. As we saw, this means that gender inequality is far more pronounced in Spain than in Scandinavia or the US. The share that is done jointly is surprisingly

[11] These effects were estimated using SURE (seemingly unrelated regression) regressions. SURE regression allows the estimation of several outcomes at the same time; in our case, child care, housework and paid employment. The advantage is that it captures the interdependence between people's daily activities: the amount of time one can devote to children is obviously constrained by how much time one dedicates to alternative tasks such as housework, leisure, or one's job.

[12] All estimations are based on OLS since this permits us to estimate marginal effects. The Tobit estimator is often preferred in time-use analysis due to the presence of censored observations. In the Spanish data, the degree of censoring is minimal. Estimations using Tobit come, in fact, to identical results. Since the inclusion of weekly paid working hours introduces potential endogeneity, the ideal would have been to estimate simultaneous regressions. The results presented here do, however, not correct for endogeneity and this may introduce some – but in all probability not disabling – bias. Correlating the residuals from SURE regressions suggests the presence of endogeneity between paid work and housework (the correlation is 0.5) but only to a limited extent between paid work and child care (the correlation is 0.2).

Table 1.4 Couple specialization in housework (minutes per day; weekdays only)

	Husband's time	Wife's time	Proportion joint time
Intercept	95.9***	297.5***	.27***
Couple variables			
Wife's bargaining power	61.0***	−81.8***	.09***
Similar productivities	−11.6***	−9.5	.02*
Homogamy	−1.2	6.3	−.02**
Homogamy* high education	1.0	−32.7***	.08***
Individual characteristics			
Education: low	5.6	−7.6	
Education: medium	9.2**	−23.7***	
Education: high	9.2	−21.5**	
N	3758	3758	7516
R-squared	.086	.339	.014

Source: INE of Spain. Significance levels: * = 0.10; ** = 0.05; *** = 0.01
Controls not shown: age, working hours, working in the public sector, the use of paid outside help, child care, and help from family members, number of children, and presence of children aged less than 6 years

large (27%), which suggests that most of men's household chores are done together with their wives. In Spain, too, we find the usual education effects: educated men chip in more; highly educated women, less. Now, what do the results tell us about the mechanisms of gender specialization?

First and foremost, wives' bargaining power appears to be the single most influential factor. The marginal effect is substantial. If the wife's relative wage rate were to double (say from 25–50% of their combined wage), this would produce a 60% increase in men's housework time and a corresponding 28% decrease in women's. The same jump would also generate a very significant (30%) increase in jointly done housework. These are, by a large margin, the strongest effects present. Having similar market productivities is of lesser consequence. It reduces males' contribution significantly, but the effect is not huge and it adds a notch to the time dedicated jointly. Indirectly, however, productivities do affect women's behaviour. More productive women sacrifice child care – and even more housework – to the benefit of paid employment. A one-standard deviation increase in women's wages produces a doubling of paid work, a 10% reduction in child care, and 27% less housework.[13] On this score, we find a marked contrast with Danish women. While they also work longer hours when they earn more, this does not affect their time with children at all. This may perhaps reflect national differences with regard to the prioritization of children, but a far more persuasive interpretation is that the trade-offs between career and motherhood are so much more severe in Spain. In any case, when we consider the overall weak effect of spousal productivities on child care and housework, we must conclude that the credibility of the traditional Becker model is not overwhelming. Put differently, we must look to preferences and power as the primary movers.

The homogamy effect, as I interpret it here, captures congruent preferences and values owing to educational matching. In general, as is evident, its influence on gender equality is negative. But when we isolate university educated homogamous couples we find, firstly, that the sign turns positive for men and negative (significantly so) for women. The logic of homogamy is clearly different at the 'top' and 'bottom'. Among the low educated, it is associated with conventional 'doing-gender' behaviour; among the highly educated, the opposite. In essence, the Spanish data confirm what Evertsson and Nermo (2007) found for Sweden, and Bonke and Esping-Andersen (2008) for Denmark. Put differently, we seem to have uncovered a phenomenon that is quite pervasive within advanced countries.

The contrast in behaviour emerges most clearly when we examine jointly performed housework. Here we see that the likelihood of doing tasks together jumps by 30% for university level homogamous couples. This does provide some support for the argument that similar preferences do pattern time use, at least among the highly educated. It also suggests the presence of a rather bipolar specialization scenario: the highly educated homogamous couples embrace more egalitarianism while the low educated remain loyal to conventional gender norms. We find

[13] Estimated from SURE regressions, not shown.

Table 1.5 Specialization in child care: child families only (minutes per day)

	Husbands	Wives	Proportion Jointly
Intercept	29.8**	143.1***	.19***
Couple variables			
Wife's bargaining power	29.0***	−21.3*	−.02
Similar productivity	−0.9	4.7	−0.01
Homogamy	−0.4	−2.5	−0.02
Homogamy*high education	10.6*	−0.8	.09***
Individual characteristics			
Education: low	0.0	14.0***	
Education medium	10.8**	20.2***	
Education: high	11.2*	38.5***	
N	2830	2830	5660
R-squared	.213	.406	.040

Source: INE of Spain. Significance levels: * = 0.10; ** = 0.05; *** = 0.01
Controls not shown: age, working hours, working in the public sector, the use of paid outside help, child care, and help from family members, number of children, and presence of children aged less than 6 years

exactly the same pattern for Danish couples (Bonke and Esping-Andersen, 2008).

Gender differences are also substantial in child care since Spanish mothers dedicate three times as much time as fathers to their children – on weekdays. We should be careful to avoid interpreting this as demonstrated lack of interest. The work day is prohibitively long for the typical Spanish male. The results in Table 1.5 suggest a specialization pattern fairly similar to the previous one. Wives' bargaining power is, as before, the principal determinant of specialization. Here the marginal effect is even larger, namely almost 100%: if she doubles her relative wage this will also double the father's childcare time (and produce a minor decrease in mothers' time as well). As before, there is no significant effect of partners' respective productivities. Perhaps the most striking finding is that the bipolar impact of homogamy emerges even more clearly in child care. Being a university educated, homogamous couple implies a 30% increase in fathers' care and, most tellingly, a substantial leap (again about 30%) in joint caring. The education gradient is, however, noticeable. Higher educated parents of both sexes contribute far more time to their children.

Indeed, the gap between low and high educated is quite huge. For the highly educated mothers, it is clear that the time gained via bargaining is more than annulled because they actively prefer to spend more time with their children.

All told, there is undoubtedly plenty of evidence in favour of the 'doing-gender' thesis – in Spain certainly more than elsewhere. But traditionalism is clearly weakened when the wife experiences a major increase in her bargaining power. When her relative earnings double, the gender gap is reduced to 30 per cent, i.e., a tenfold reduction in spousal specialization. In addition, her bargaining power increases the joint time substantially. This indicates that conventional 'doing-gender' practices erode in tandem with women's attainment of greater economic autonomy.

It would seem that not even Spanish couples adhere very much to the precepts of Becker's theory of specialization. Differences or similarities of spousal market productivity matter very little for the allocation of domestic tasks. But neither does the 'doing-gender' thesis receive unequivocal support. To begin with, bargaining does play a decisive role. Secondly, we see a very bi-modal pattern of spousal decision-making: the low educated may exhibit conventional gender roles; the highly educated are unquestionably moving towards gender equality.

The analyses of time spent together on domestic chores and, in particular, on child care reveal that shared preferences and values among the highly educated produce behaviour that directly contradicts the standard specialization *and* also the 'doing-gender' theses.

In general, the behavioural characteristics of families appear rather polarized across the population. This, I believe, is as good an indicator as any of the stage at which, in this case the Spanish, female revolution has reached. The large gap in parenting between the low- and high-educated suggests, moreover, that such discrepancies will have ripple effects on children's developmental prospects. The gap between low- and high-educated parents' caring time is roughly 30 per cent in Denmark, the US and Spain. And both the Danish and the US data suggest that the gap has been rising over the past decade. We shall revisit these issues in chapter 2 and then again in chapter 4.

The Incomplete Revolution

The weight of the evidence does perhaps lean in favour of 'revolutionary' change in the way women, and perhaps also men, behave. Yet, it is not difficult to identify corners of society, sometimes large ones, where people remain quite faithful to traditional gender norms. We see this in the allocation of domestic tasks, in employment behaviour and also in marital choices. We also see it in the way that women express their views on family life.

The traditional family-oriented woman, following Hakim's (1996) typology, is clearly still very much present in our societies. A 'traditional male breadwinner' preference is arguably the best identifier of conventional preferences. Believing that mothers should remain home with pre-school children is somewhat ambiguous since a 'yes' may simply imply that mothers care intensely about their child's welfare. If we therefore focus on the breadwinner preference, Table 1.6 reveals, unsurprisingly, that traditional gender norms have largely disappeared from Swedish society. What is surprising is that a quarter of American women appear traditional, just like in Spain – a prototypical revolutionary laggard. Scott (2008: Table 6.1) presents a rare over-time profile of gendered attitudes for Britain, showing that women and men have moved significantly in an egalitarian direction over the past decades. On most dimensions women display stronger egalitarian views except, curiously enough, for dual-income arrangements. In any case, the dynamics undoubtedly point towards a decisive break with conventional norms regarding women's place in the family. Scott's data for other countries show pretty much the same trend, but with one important rider: the leap in egalitarian lifestyle preferences is unusually steep in laggard countries like Ireland, the Netherlands and Spain (Scott, 2008: Table 6.2). And her data on cohort-specific attitudes confirm my earlier suggestion that the revolutionary momentum of the female revolution is particularly evident among higher educated women from the baby-boom generation onwards.

The female revolution has evolved in a clearly stratified manner, beginning with higher educated, middle-class women. Comparing across the OECD countries, we find rather similar patterns of gender employment parity within this group. The degree to which the female revolution nears completion is essentially a question of how much less educated women, or women married to less educated men, have followed suit. Among women with no more than obligatory schooling, the employment rate is about 60–65% in the Nordic countries and a bit lower in the US. But it drops to 27% in Italy and to 35% in Southern Europe on average. Here, of course, we need to remember that the share of low-educated women is small indeed in Scandinavia (and the US) but rather substantial in Southern Europe.

Table 1.6 Women's gender role preferences

	Favour traditional male breadwinner family (%)	Believe that it is best that mothers remain home with pre-school kids (%)
Germany (W)	23	56
Ireland	19	36
Netherlands	12	40
Spain	25	52
Sweden	8	24
UK	20	39
US	24	38

Source: International Social Survey Programme: Social Inequality III (ISSP 2002), distributed by GESIS Data Archive, ZA3880

Women's greater investment in education mirrors, without doubt, their commitment to lifetime autonomy and the pursuit of good jobs. Goldin et al. (2006) argue that it also reflects the fact that women reap higher returns from education than do men. But overall levels of education must be interpreted with caution since women continue to select themselves into conventionally female fields of study that offer inferior earnings prospects, such as the humanities or nursing. In fact, the gender bias in fields of study seems to explain a substantial amount of the wage gap among graduates (Gregory, 2008).

Overall employment rates fail, however, to convey fully the degree to which women have achieved parity with men in the labour market. There are, in particular, two qualifiers to be considered. One, how stable is participation across women's entire life cycle? In the past, the typical woman would interrupt or completely abandon employment around the first birth. As discussed earlier, there has been a sharp decline in women's birth-related interruptions in Britain. But low-educated women, nonetheless, continue to exit for several years (Dex et al., 2008). For the US, Blau et al. (1998) show that a typical woman in the 1950s and 1960s lost seven working years during the fertile ages 25–40. Interestingly, this had hardly changed by 1980. But all available evidence suggests that work interruptions are now fewer – because of lower fertility – and shorter. The most recent data show that the employment rate of mothers with children less than 2 years of age is only marginally lower than for women generally in Canada, France, the US and Scandinavia. The gap is quite huge in Germany where women continue to interrupt for extended periods (Gauthier and Lelievre, 1994; OECD, 2007). And most countries present an essentially bi-modal pattern of work inter-ruptions: few and very brief among the highly educated; more and significantly longer among the less educated. US data illustrate this well. While 60% of college-educated mothers return within one year of giving birth, this is only so for 18% of those with less than high school qualifications (US Census Bureau, 2005: Table 5).

Towards the end of working life, women have traditionally faced the necessity of caring for frail old parents. This meant either a major disincentive to return to work as the children matured, or it implied a – usually irreversible – second career interruption. Sarasa and Mestres (2005) show that only 3% of Danish women who care for another report that this prevents them from working, compared to 13% in Germany, 22% in the UK and a full one-quarter of all in Spain.

The second qualifier lies in part-time employment which can be seen to represent a more cautious step into the world of work. Part-time work has almost everywhere been a hallmark of the early stages of women's transition. It has, unsurprisingly, grown very rapidly in the laggard countries, such as Germany, the Netherlands, Italy and Spain. In countries where the female revolution is most mature – Scandinavia – it has experienced a noticeable decline in past decades. As in North America, the majority of women are, and remain throughout most of their careers, full-timers (OECD, 2007). Indeed, as I noted earlier, part-time in Denmark is now primarily a temporary bridge between maternity leave and resumed full-time work. Here again, the level of education makes a decisive difference. As Blossfeld and Hakim (1997) demonstrate, the part-time option is far more prevalent among women in lower grade jobs. This same group of women is also far more likely to work part-time for extended periods of their careers.

The intensity of labour supply affects women's economic autonomy and power within the couple. The economic dominance of husbands has of course abated. In the US, the share of couples in which the male is sole provider has been cut in half – from 60% in 1970 to less than 30% today. But the trend looks less 'revolutionary' when we examine households in terms of husbands providing the majority (60% plus) or all of their income. In this case, the decline is from 88% to 70%. Husbands' income dominance is, unsurprisingly, far more accentuated in couples where the wife's education is low (Raley et al., 2006). In a broader nation comparison, Bianchi et al. (1996) find that women's earnings dependency has become basically marginal in Sweden, but continues to represent roughly 30% in the US, and half of all women (or more) in the continental European countries.

The revolution of women's roles is incomplete in different ways. The masculinization of women's biographies is far more pronounced in economic behaviour than in family life. Hochchild's (1989) argument that the revolution has stalled in the domestic sphere may appear wildly exaggerated in light of the non-trivial gender equalization that has taken place. Gershuny et al.'s (1994) notion of a lagged adaptation seems to capture ongoing trends far better. Secondly, the revolution appears highly stratified; far less so in the Nordic countries where it clearly has gone further than anywhere else; more so in countries where it is still in its infancy. This will have major repercussions throughout society. In chapter 2, I shall show that gender equalization, if it is incomplete and highly stratified, will paradoxically nurture more societal inequality. And in chapter 4, I shall show that the more incomplete the revolution, the more likely it is that we shall see polarizing tendencies in terms of parenting and children's life chances.

But the data also tell us that there is one basic preference that has not been affected by the revolution: all evidence suggests that the quest for motherhood remains strong. As a result, one of the greatest tensions in modern society has to do with the reconciliation of careers and motherhood. Indeed, women's revolution is likely to produce adverse consequences for family life as well as for society at large unless it finds support from the welfare state. This is the question that will be explored in the next chapter.

2

The New Inequalities

The revolution in women's roles and the maturation of the knowledge economy both contribute to the creation of economic wealth and social innovation. But they also give rise to new social risks and inequalities. Polarization is a strong word but, as I shall argue in this chapter, we do face polarizing trends along a host of dimensions. Firstly, we are witnessing a tidal wave of rising income inequality. This can be traced to changes in the economic returns to skills, to changes in family structure and also to the (incomplete) female revolution. Secondly, there are signs that society is polarizing between work-rich and work-poor households. Thirdly, the intensity of risks in traditionally vulnerable groups, such as lone mothers, is likely to worsen since divorce patterns and lone motherhood are increasingly biased towards low-educated populations. Finally, and very much correlated with the above, we see signs that parental investments in children are also becoming more unequal. A paradox of our epoch is that the quest for gender equality may very well produce greater societal inequalities if the quest is strongest among high-status women. In most countries this is exactly the case.

Rising Income Inequality

Ours is an epoch of rising inequalities. Many commentators speak of a 'great U-turn': after decades of income compression we now register major reversals. With only one or two exceptions, all OECD countries have experienced widening income differentials over the past decades; in some cases, like the UK and the

US, dramatically so (Forster and D'Ercole, 2005). Most of the burgeoning literature traces it to changes in the labour market, particularly to rising skills premiums, eroding trade union power, employment deregulation and unemployment. US data indicate that the wage returns to additional years of schooling have almost doubled since 1980 (Juhn et al., 1993; Katz and Autor, 1999; Morris and Western, 1999; Ryscavage, 1999; Kenworthy and Pontusson, 2005).

The great U-turn is best understood on the backdrop of the post-war income compression (Levy, 1998; Davies and Shorrocks, 1999). As Karoly and Burtless (1995) show, 40 per cent of the reduction in income inequality in the 1960s was due to declining earnings inequality among male heads of families. The tide lifted all boats but gave the little boats an extra lift.

A perusal of trends since the 1970s invites gloom. At first, rising inequality appeared restricted to the UK and the US (Gottschalk and Smeeding, 1997; Atkinson, 1999). Hence, the phenomenon appeared idiosyncratic rather than global, a consequence of these countries' unregulated labour markets and weak unions (Katz and Autor, 1999). But now we see that most countries are following suit – including traditional bastions of strong labour movements and social equality such as Scandinavia.

The growth in market income inequality between 1980 and 2000 is shown in Table 2.1. The rise in the Gini coefficient is virtually everywhere substantial, most dramatic in the UK, but we also note with surprise the leap in inequality in Sweden. Predictably, the trend is far less dramatic when we turn to disposable incomes. Kenworthy and Pontusson (2005) argue that welfare states intensified redistribution in response to widening inequalities. But this is not true for Sweden, Italy and the US where the rise in the disposable (after taxes and transfers) income Gini is pretty much the same as for market incomes.

The U-turn is very much driven by the top pulling ahead of the rest which, of course, attests to the widening earnings differentials (Katz and Autor, 1999; Gottschalk and Smeeding, 1997). The ratio between the top and middle deciles rose from 1.8 to 2.2 in Britain; from 2.6 to 3.0 in the US; and from 1.5 to 1.7 in Sweden. But the bottom is losing ground, too, in the US, Finland, Germany,

Table 2.1 Changes in household income inequality over the 1980s and 1990s

	Market Incomes			Disposable Incomes		
	Gini 1980	Gini 2000	% change	Gini 1980	Gini 2000	% change
Denmark	.331	.355	+6	.254	.266	+4
Norway	.284	.337	+19	.223	.251	+13
Sweden	.293	.375	+28	.197	.252	+28
France	.395	.403	+1	.270	.273	0
Germany	.285	.360	+26	.244	.264	+8
Italy*	.434	.456	+7	.306	.333	+9
Spain	n.a.	.574	n.a.	.318	.323	+2
UK	.332	.450	+36	.270	.345	+28
US	.359	.436	+21	.301	.368	+22

Sources: Luxembourg Income Study (LIS) data, and Kenworthy and Pontusson (2005: Table A2)
*Italian and Danish data are OECD estimates for 1985 and 2000 and derive from Forster and d'Ercole (2005: Table 4). The Spanish 2000 estimates are from the ECHP

Italy, Sweden and the UK. Considering the magnitudes, de facto polarization seems limited to the UK and US.[1]

Young adults bear much of the brunt, facing an erosion of relative wages at all skill levels while being hugely overrepresented among the unemployed and those with precarious, short-term employment contracts (Wasmer, 2002; Polavieja, 2003). More broadly, the relative disposable income of young adults (18–25) has declined by 7 percentage points on average in the OECD (Forster and d'Ercole, 2005: Annex Table A6). Surprisingly, the young have suffered an especially steep decline in the Nordic countries.

The deteriorating position of young workers and the rise in lone parenthood help account for growing child poverty. The Nordic welfare states have succeeded in stemming the tide but elsewhere child poverty has risen sharply: by 4–7 percentage points in Germany, the Netherlands, Italy, and the UK; and the

[1] Smeeding (2004: Table 1) shows that between 1979 and 2000, the lowest fifth in the US gained a total of $1,100 (or 9 per cent) in real terms while the top fifth gained a whopping $576,400 (or 201 per cent).

US, starting at a very high level (19 per cent in 1980), saw child poverty growing by an additional 3 points.[2]

The new inequalities are, no doubt, driven by ongoing labour market transformation (OECD, 2000). On one hand, high unemployment contributes to inequality and helps in particular to account for the eroding status of young adults. New school leavers will, in many EU countries, face protracted unemployment periods. In Italy and Spain, the average youth unemployment spell is 23 months which compares unfavourably with Denmark (5 months) and the UK's 6 months (OECD, 2007). On the other hand, the rising returns to skills include also an experience component which penalizes younger workers (Katz and Autor, 1999).

The inegalitarian consequences of new technologies very much depend, however, on trends in the supply of skills. Acemoglu (2002) and also Goldin and Katz (2008) argue that university enrolments in the US have, since the 1970s, lagged behind the demand for strong skills, producing extraordinarily high-skill premiums. In Europe the opposite occurred: the supply of highly educated workers has outpaced technological change and this, in turn, has put a brake on wages at the top of the skill pyramid. Nonetheless, there is a clear overrepresentation of young workers within the low-wage population throughout Europe. Lucifora et al. (2005) show that about 60% of youth (under 25) are low-waged in the Netherlands and the UK, and about 40% in France and Germany. These are very large numbers, however interpreted.

But not all news is gloomy. Although the female wage distribution follows the male trend, the gender wage gap is closing at all skill levels. Wage erosion at the bottom is far worse among low-skilled males while highly skilled women enjoy major earnings gains relative to similar men (Blau and Kahn, 2003; Waldfogel and Mayer, 1999). And the 'youth-penalty', too, is biased against males. In the US, the earnings of 25–34-year-old males declined by 23% compared to only 4.5% among women during the 1980s and 1990s (Schrammel, 1998).

Trends in the gender pay gap vary substantially across countries (Blau and Kahn, 2003: Table 7.2; OECD, 2002: Tables 2.15

---

[2] Estimated from LIS data.

and 2.16). The latest Eurostat data show that it has narrowed substantially in the UK, the Netherlands, Ireland and Italy. It has remained basically stable in Denmark, France and Germany, but it has also widened – and appreciably so – in Spain and even Sweden.[3] If women enjoy relative pay gains and simultaneously work more, their contribution to total household income will rise. In France, the Netherlands and Spain their relative income contribution rose by a full 5 percentage points. The result is that the gender composition of total household income is becoming less asymmetric, in Denmark approaching parity. In countries with lower female labour supply, like the Netherlands and Spain, their share hovers around 25 per cent.[4]

The Impact of Changing Demographics

There are three great demographic transformations that can influence income distributions. Firstly, rising marital instability implies more vulnerable units – lone-parent families in particular. Karoly and Burtless (1995) find that the rise of female-headed households explains about half of the total increase in the US Gini during the 1970s and 1980s. The share of children in single-mother households now ranges from a low of 5% in Southern Europe to a high of 15–20% in Scandinavia and North America.[5]

Secondly, marital homogamy in terms of education, especially at the high end, affects households' combined earnings power and is likely to accentuate inequalities (Blossfeld and Drobnic, 2001; Burtless, 1999).[6] But the effect of marital selection depends on the third transformation, namely on the intensity of female labour supply.

If labour supply is positively correlated with education, female employment will almost certainly enhance inequalities. To put

---

[3] Eurostat data from *NewCronos*.

[4] The only exceptions are Germany and the UK. Calculations are based on the European Community Household Panel (ECHP), waves 1994–2001.

[5] Estimates from LIS Key Figures (www.lisproject.org/keyfigures).

[6] The correlation for couples' education ranges from 0.5 in Denmark, Germany, and the UK, to 0.6+ in Italy, Sweden and the US (estimated from Canada Statistics IALS micro-data files).

it simply, the high-skilled double-earner couple will race ahead of the rest, especially if joblessness is more widespread at the bottom. In contrast, if female labour supply were to grow faster at the 'low end', the net effect should be declining income inequality. The participation rate of less educated women is usually far below their more educated sisters, but the gap is far greater in Southern Europe than in Scandinavia, the UK, or the US.

As I shall show below, there are clear signs that American women in the lower end of the income distribution have increased labour supply so as to offset the deteriorating earnings of low-skilled males. This reflects the traditional labour supply response among women. And if it primarily represents compensatory behaviour due to eroding male earnings, it is unlikely to have any major equalizing effects.

Since unemployment tends to come in couples, marital homogamy will contribute to polarization (Gregg and Wadsworth, 2001). The share of working-age *couples* with no employed adult varies from 6–8% in Scandinavia, Germany and the US to 13–15% in the UK and the Netherlands.[7] The income gap between work-poor and work-rich households will be especially large in countries – like those in Southern Europe – where dual-career couples are mainly found at the top, or in countries like the US where welfare state support is ungenerous.

So, even if less educated women increase their participation, an equalizing effect may still fail to materialize if there are major asymmetries in the intensity of employment. To illustrate, a two-career couple may potentially supply 80 or perhaps even 100 hours per week; the single earner half that; and the lone mother, realistically far less. Evidence suggests that such asymmetries are widening (Juhn and Murphy, 1997; Aaronson, 2002; Karoly and Burtless, 1995). Smeeding's (2004) data for Europe and North America show that couples in the top quintile work roughly two to three times as many annual hours as do the lowest, and about 20–30% more hours than does the middle quintile. Hyslop (2001) shows that assortative mating accounts for 23% of the rise in US household income inequality.

---

[7] The figures would be far higher were we to include also single person and lone-parent households (see OECD, 1998: Table 1.7).

Table 2.2 Homogamy of labour supply and earnings: couple correlations for
1993 and 2001

	1993	1993	2001	2001
	Labour supply	Earnings	Labour supply	Earnings
Denmark	.39	.20	.41	.16
France	.26	.19	.22	.17
Germany	.19	−.13	.20	−.12
Italy	.17	.15	.17	.18
Spain	.12	.18	.18	.20
Sweden	n.a.	.52	.17	
UK	.31	.16	.32	.07
US	.27	.10	.29	.07

Source: ECHP, panels 1994 and 2001 and, for the US, PSID panels for same years

A key empirical question, therefore, is whether educational
homogamy spills over to labour supply and earnings. We can estimate this by simple couple correlations of (weekly) hours worked
and of (annual) work income[8] (see Table 2.2).

Labour supply homogamy is, unsurprisingly, stronger in high
female-participation countries, such as Denmark and Sweden,
and correspondingly weaker in Italy and Spain. Yet, similarities of
work intensity may not produce high (annual-based) earnings correlations simply because women are more likely to interrupt their
careers. But the discrepancy is surely also due to compositional
factors. Even if female employment is low, the Spanish earnings
correlations are high because women in top-level occupations
are married to men in similar high-status jobs (Smith, 2005).
Germany's negative earnings correlations suggest that wives of
very high-income men work very little.

The Female Revolution and Inequality

The revolutionary change in women's roles may, then, be a mixed
blessing if either directly or indirectly it produces greater societal inequality. A surge in inequality will influence not only the

---

[8] The correlations refer to couple households and include zero earnings and/or
zero hours worked.

distribution of living standards today but may also affect the opportunity structure for subsequent generations. The more unequal is family income, the greater the inequalities in parental investment in their children (Solon, 1999).[9] On this backdrop it is evidently of some importance to identify more precisely how changes in women's economic behaviour affect the income distribution and, indirectly, parents' capacity to invest in their children.

There are surprisingly few studies that have broached this question systematically and the existing literature is mostly based on US data.[10] There are several factors that can dictate how female employment influences inequalities. *Firstly*, the effect depends on the distribution of women across household types, in particular with regard to couple units relative to single-person (and lone-mother) households. As noted, US research finds that the rise in single-mother families has contributed significantly to inequality. The distribution of women across household types is patterned by demographic factors such as age, race and education. For instance, single-parenthood rates in the US are approximately three times higher among blacks than whites (Ellwood and Jencks, 2004). The actual effect will depend on the kinds of social selection mechanisms at play: in some countries (like the UK and the US), lone motherhood is associated with low education and high poverty risks. The recent fall in teenage births in the US may, however, offset part of this selection effect. In Scandinavia, such selection mechanisms should be weaker, in part because most lone mothers work and in part because they receive generous welfare state support. They should, likewise, be less accentuated in Southern Europe, but for different reasons since the high cost of divorce implies that it is very much a higher social status affair. Yet, if we include also cohabiting couples in the analysis, the impact of changing family structure appears weaker (Martin, 2006).

Secondly, if we restrict ourselves to couple households, the effect will depend on *which* women increase their labour supply

---

[9] Parental income is, of course, only one among many factors that influence children's life chances. In fact, as I argue in chapter 4, non-monetary dimensions of parenthood may be more decisive.

[10] For a European focus, see Maitre et al. (2003) and Esping-Andersen (2007).

Table 2.3 Women's role in household income: couples aged 25–59

	Earnings ratio:Top/bottom quintile			How much (%) do wives increase household labour supply?	
	Men	Women	Household	Top income quintile	Bottom income quintile
Denmark	5.8	4.3	5.2	82	80
France	5.7	8.5	6.3	78	72
Germany	4.1	4.8	4.3	72	68
Ireland	9.3	12.0	9.7	62	65
Netherlands	5.2	7.7	5.7	62	52
Spain	8.8	23.2	10.6	80	82
UK	7.0	5.3	6.4	73	59

Source: Estimations based on the European Community Household Panel data (Wave 6) © European Communities 1994–2009

and earnings most. If most of the increase is concentrated among higher educated women, or among women married to high-earning men, the impact is likely to be inegalitarian. If we see a major increase in single-mother employment, the effect should be equalizing (Western et al., 2008).

Table 2.3 presents one way of assessing the inegalitarian effects of women's employment and earnings across *couple* households. To exclude students and retirees, I focus on couples aged 25–59. I calculate the earnings ratio for men and women respectively in the top and bottom earnings quintile. If the earnings ratio is steeper among women than men, we would conclude that wives' earnings augment inequality between households. We can gauge the same effect by comparing the male ratio with the total household ratio. If the latter is higher than the former, we conclude that wives' contribution produces inequality. Table 2.3 also highlights the gaps related to wives' employment level.

Among the countries included, we see that wives' labour supply (measured in weekly hours) is far less intensive in the bottom quintile households than in the top. The gap is especially pronounced in the Netherlands and the UK, two countries with a very high rate of female part-timers. In Denmark, Ireland and

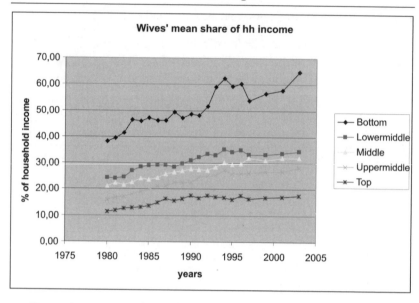

Figure 2.1 Wives' share of household income by men's quintile:
United States
Note: 'Wives' include also cohabiting women
Source: 1980–2004 Panel Study of Income Dynamics

Spain there are no real differences in labour supply across the quintiles. Turning now to income distribution effects, we find that women's earnings produce more inequality in all countries but Denmark and the UK – and most dramatically so in Ireland and Spain. This reflects the fact that, in these two countries, women in the bottom quintile earn very little and often have zero earnings.

Such cross-sectional snapshots, however, do not provide an adequate answer to our question which in essence is a dynamic one: what is the impact of the *rise* in women's employment over the past decades? To capture the dynamics, I turn to the US for which we have long-term panel data. Here we witness a clear rise in women's contribution to total household income (see Figure 2.1). The increase has been in the order of 50% across the quintiles and, with the exception of the very top and bottom, wives' contribution now hovers around 30% of the total. This is somewhat greater than in most EU countries, but is also considerably lower than the

Scandinavian share. The role of wives' income has been especially marked in the lowest quintile of male earnings where their share now exceeds 60% of the total. This basically reflects a compensatory behaviour in light of the deteriorating position of low-skilled males in the US labour market (Juhn and Murphy, 1997).

This leads us to the female and male wage distribution. The gender wage gap has narrowed in tandem with the rise in women's employment, fewer children and shorter birth interruptions (Blau and Kahn, 2003; Waldfogel and Mayer, 1999). But it has been narrowing at different rates. In the Nordic countries, the gap has been stable among high-skilled women and has continued to close among the less skilled. This, conditional on male-partner earnings, should favour an equalizing trend. In the US the opposite occurred in the 1990s. And if, as in the US, less skilled male earnings are eroding, the effect will be compounded – in particular where marital homogamy is the norm.

The connection between female employment and inequality depends, as the *fourth* factor, also on how households fare across the business cycle. This has, surprisingly, not been given much attention. Yet, when we examine year-by-year changes in female employment, it is noticeable how women in general, and less educated women in particular, are vulnerable to economic slowdowns. In a previous study, I conducted year-by-year variance decompositions of changes in household inequality and the results suggest that the impact of women's earnings on total household income distribution tends to be more inegalitarian in recession years. One way to interpret this is that women coupled to low-wage men (usually low-skilled women) are disproportionately vulnerable to unemployment (first fired, last hired). Once again we see the repercussions of assortative mating (Esping-Andersen, 2007).

The *fifth* factor is partnership formation in the broader sense. On one hand, as already discussed, marital selection in terms of human capital attributes can have substantial effects. On the other hand, there are no doubt selection mechanisms behind the dynamics of coupling and uncoupling. Those who remain single, or become so, are not necessarily similar to those who form couples. The overall effect of partnering is difficult to predict. We would expect that singlehood is more predominant among women seriously dedicated to careers, or among women who face poor marriage markets. As mentioned, divorce and lone motherhood are in some countries an upper-class affair; in others biased towards the bottom.

Disentangling the Link Between Women's Employment and Inequality

The three basic factors that need to be disentangled are: (1) stratified patterns of divorce; (2) the role of assortative mating; and (3) the proliferation of single-earner versus dual-earner families. To show this I will focus on the US case, in part because it provides the kind of good long-term panel data that is required; and in part because the US exemplifies very well the unfolding female revolution.

The probabilities of divorce will, if they differ across social strata, have consequences for inequality. In Figure 2.2, I plot the survival rate of marriages by families' income quintile over a 25-year span. The differences in marital stability are noteworthy. After 10 years, 30% of low-income couples are divorced, compared to only 15% in the top quintile. After 20 years, the gap widens to 20 percentage points.

This kind of social bias will have major effects both for the income distribution and probably for child welfare as well. As I shall show subsequently, single-motherhood rates have been stable over the past decades among highly educated women. They have practically doubled among the low educated. If low-income populations are far more likely to divorce and subsequently form single-person, or lone-parent, units, this clearly creates an exceptionally vulnerable family segment at the bottom of the income distribution. And this will most likely affect parental investment in children as well.

As we also saw in chapter 1, patterns of marital selection are changing. The traditional model of male 'supremacy' (hypergamy) is declining. In the US it now represents less than a quarter of all couples. Homogamy, on the other hand, has risen but primarily at the top of the income pyramid. If we go back to 1980, there were no real differences in homogamy but twenty years later the gap between the top and the bottom quintiles exceeds 10 percentage points (see Figure 2.3).

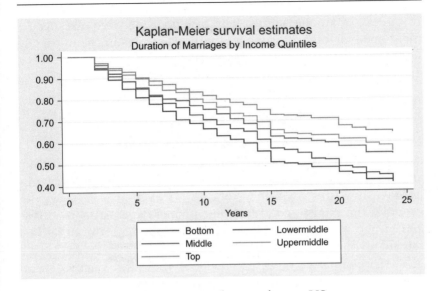

Figure 2.2 Marital survival rates: US

Data source: PSID (Population Study of Income Dynamics) waves 1980–2003

And dual-earner couples have risen everywhere, but at a different pace. They now account for almost 70% of all couple households in Scandinavia and between 40% and 50% in most EU countries. In the US, the main jump occurred in the 1980s, rising from 54% in 1980 to 68% in 1990; thereafter the rate has levelled off. Families that depend solely on a male breadwinner are in rapid decline.

The share of zero-earning wives has fallen below 20% in the US. The key issue is of course where in the male income distribution these zero-earner women are concentrated. Here we find that they are primarily concentrated at the top and the bottom. This, one would expect, would also promote a widening gap between the bottom and the rest.

Indeed, such potential polarization is also brought out if we examine households where there is only one earner more generally, be it male or female. In the US, the rate of single-earner couples has remained fairly stable, at 40%, at the bottom, but declined markedly in all the middle quintiles.

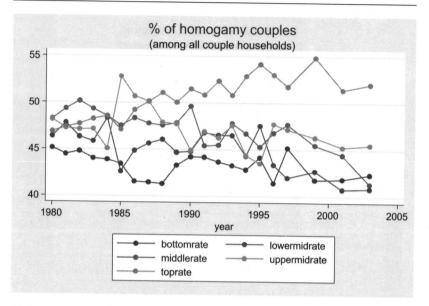

Figure 2.3 Trends in marital homogamy in the US by income quintiles
Data source: PSID (Population Study of Income Dynamics) waves 1980–2003

If dual earnership is far more prevalent in the top quintiles, this will add to inequality. But the effect depends naturally on how much the couples work. In Figures 2.4 and 2.5, I present, respectively, the trends in dual-earner couples and the rate of part-time work among wives, once again comparing across income quintiles.

In the US, dual earning is the norm in all couples except in the bottom quintile. This should produce more polarization. But we also see that women married to high-income men are more likely to be part-timers while those married to low-wage men are more likely to be full-timers. This certainly suggests the presence of compensatory strategies that should weaken any inegalitarian impulses that may come from homogamy and from dual earnership.

Simulation techniques offer one method of pinpointing the overall effect of women's earnings on the income distribution. Basically we construct a counterfactual of what the overall income distribution in *t+* would have looked like had there been no change in *quintile-specific* female employment or, alternatively,

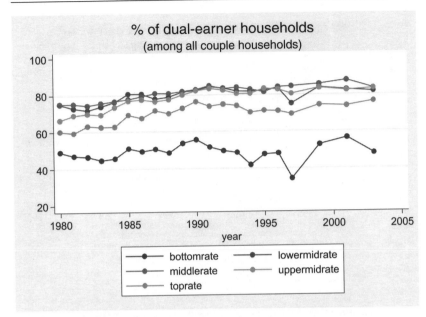

Figure 2.4 Percentage of dual-earner couples in the US
Data source: PSID (Population Study of Income Dynamics) waves 1980–2003

what would inequality have looked like had women in the bottom quintile behaved like women at the top.

The first row in Table 2.4 shows the *actual* trend in the Gini coefficient among couple households. The simulations suggest that female labour supply in the top (male) quintiles, but especially in the fifth, is decisive for inequality. Had it not risen over the two decades, the Gini in 2003 would have been about 7 per cent lower.

Can changes in female employment at the bottom offset the inegalitarian impulse from the top? To answer this question I include three simulations. Row 4 holds constant the labour supply of bottom-quintile women, but this hardly alters the level of inequality at all. But if, as rows 5 and 6 suggest, bottom-quintile women had experienced a rise in labour supply identical to the fifth quintile, this would have produced a non-trivial 3 per cent reduction in inequality. If this had in fact occurred, it would have helped offset the inegalitarian thrust that comes from the high-quintile households.

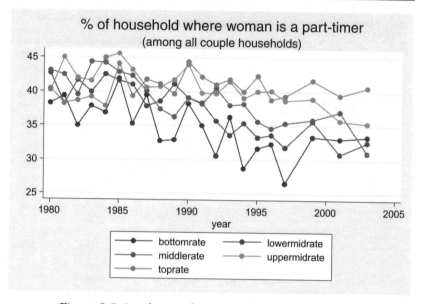

Figure 2.5 Incidence of wives working part-time: US
Data source: PSID (Population Study of Income Dynamics) waves 1980–2003

In other words, this exercise confirms very much the basic point that an incomplete revolution of women's roles is likely to produce great income inequalities. And it pinpoints quite well where, precisely, the frontiers of the revolution are drawn. The top may, as we have seen, be racing away from the rest in terms of income. The US example suggests that the consequence would be far less polarizing were bottom-end women also to embrace the revolution.

Polarization and Social Welfare

The new waves of income inequality that arrive on the shores of the rich nations are the by-products of the rising returns to skills, and also of earnings erosion and high unemployment rates among the low skilled. The knowledge economy may be the midwife of social polarization unless we manage to diminish differences in abilities within the working-age population. Remedying skill deficiencies among adults is, however, difficult and costly. The

Table 2.4 Simulating the effects of counterfactual labour supply scenarios: couple families in the US

	1980	2003	% change
1 Initial GINI coefficient	0.321	0.401	24.92%
2 Holding constant labour supply of women in the 4th quintile	0.321	0.392	22.12%
3 Holding constant labour supply of women in the top (5th) quintile	0.321	0.373	16.20%
4 Holding constant labour supply of women in the bottom quintile	0.321	0.400	24.61%
5 Women in the bottom quintile behave like the ones in the top	0.321	0.388	20.87%
6 Women in the bottom quintile behave like the ones in the 4th	0.321	0.392	22.12%

Data source: PSID panels 1980–2003

real objective must, accordingly, be to ensure that the coming generations will possess the skills that meet the demands of the knowledge economy.

The challenge is so much the greater when we recognize that many of the new demographic trends associated with women's new roles contribute additionally to inequality. The life chances of children are affected when lone motherhood is biased towards the bottom of society while high-earning dual-career couples are concentrated in the upper half of the income distribution.

To begin with, widening income inequalities affect the resources that parents can mobilize to invest in their children's future. As I shall discuss in more detail in chapter 4, the correlation between parents' and their offspring's (when adult) income is generally strong, but particularly strong in unequal societies. This tells us that prevailing levels of income inequality in the parental generation affect children's mobility chances: the greater the inequality, the less mobility there is (Solon, 1999). Tellingly, the Gini coefficient of parental spending on children in the US has risen quite sharply (from 0.54 to 0.61) over the past decades (McLanahan, 2004). As Jantti et al. (2006) show, intergenerational upward *and* downward mobility is far greater in egalitarian societies, such as the Nordic, and especially low in the United States. And we also have research that shows that US mobility has been declining in tandem with rising inequality since the 1970s (Harding et al., 2005). The image of the United States as a land of equal opportunities is increasingly far off the mark.

The United States exhibits, on virtually all counts, far greater inequalities than in any EU member state. When, therefore, we examine how different dimensions of inequality combine, it is hardly surprising that the US appears especially polarizing. This is certainly the case with regard to parenting and child development. The rising inequalities in monetary expenditure on children are matched by growing gaps in parental time investment. The difference between college- and non-college-educated parents' primary care involvement is substantial and widening. The former now dedicate 33% more time to their children than the latter (calculated from Bianchi et al.'s (2004) data. We find similar (widening) gaps in European countries, too. The equivalent caring gap is, in Denmark, 27%, which is substantially greater than in the 1980s (Bonke and Esping-Andersen, 2008). For Spain, I find an education gap of 10% among women and 25% among men.

And where, as in the United States, lone parenthood is exceptionally skewed towards low-educated mothers, we would expect that this, too, adds fuel to a polarizing trend. From analyses of the PISA data – to be discussed in greater detail in chapter 4 – this comes out quite clearly. The PISA test gap between children of lone mothers and other children is more than 40 points in the US compared to 25 points in Denmark, and only about 10 points in Germany.[11]

There is, finally, a particular feature inherent in intergenerational mobility that promotes polarization, namely that the link between parental and offspring income is non-linear (Couch and Lillard, 2004). Put differently, it is exceptionally strong at the very bottom and the very top of the income pyramid. This can be illustrated with Jantti et al.'s (2006) data on immobility: the likelihood that sons remain in the same income bracket as their fathers. In Table 2.5 I compare two Scandinavian countries with the UK

---

[11] The PISA studies test literacy, problem-solving and quantitative skills among 15-year-olds in OECD countries. The data can be obtained directly (and free of cost) from the OECD.

Table 2.5 Probability that sons end up in their father's income quintile
(percentages)

	Denmark	Sweden	UK	US
Father's quintile:				
Bottom	25	26	30	42
Middle	22	22	19	26
Top	36	37	35	36

Source: Jantti et al. (2006)

and the US, the latter representing the high end in international inequality rankings.

These figures bring out very well the asymmetrical patterns of intergenerational social inheritance. The probability of staying in the same bracket as one's father is, in all countries, highest in the bottom and top. The 'top' offspring appear to be very well cushioned against downward mobility in all countries. Were we to imagine that sons' income prospects were completely independent of origin, then we would only expect that 20 per cent of 'top sons' would have reached the top themselves. The sons of privilege are evidently overrepresented in the top income bracket. The most interesting pattern in Table 2.5 is, however, found in the bottom quintile group. The intergenerational perpetuation of low income is clearly far stronger in the UK, and especially in the US. Indirectly, these data also reveal an interesting feature of the Nordic welfare states, namely that their equalizing effects are almost entirely directed to low-income clientele. They do not prevent the rich from passing on privilege to succeeding generations. But they do seem quite capable of sponsoring more mobility out of the bottom.

The upshot is that more unequal income distributions may contribute to worsening the opportunity structure. If we conceptualize intergenerational mobility in income terms, as Table 2.5 also does, the degree of inequality within a generation will essentially depend on two factors: one, on the monetary returns to human capital within that generation and, two, on the level of inequality that existed in the previous, parental generation. This means, in turn, that the pursuit of more equality of opportunities will require less wage dispersion in the 'child generation' and/or less income inequality in the parental generation. Since it is pretty evident that the obstacles to equality of opportunity are very much centred at the bottom and top of society, this suggests that our primary policy attention should be devoted to the fate of children who come from the least and most privileged social backgrounds. In chapter 3, I shall examine how welfare state reform, in particular regarding family policy, can help minimize the inegalitarian consequences of the female revolution. And chapter 4 is dedicated to what is arguably our single greatest challenge, namely how to invest optimally in our children so as to diminish the adverse consequences of strong social inheritance mechanisms.

Part II Welfare State Adaptation

3

Adapting Family Policy to the Female Revolution

Parents create, all at once, private and collective welfare. In turn, their ability to do so depends very much on how society supports the family. The increasingly large gap between the desired number of children and actual fertility must be interpreted as a blatant case of welfare failure for families themselves and also for the community they live in. The new low-fertility equilibrium that we see in many advanced countries poses, accordingly, a policy challenge of considerable urgency.

An optimal policy needs to address both n and q, to use Gary Becker's terminology for the quantity and quality of children, respectively (Becker and Lewis, 1973). Such policy will need to consider at least four issues: one, the obstacles to parenthood in the first place; two, the uneven capacity of parents to invest in their children; three, the impact of mothers' employment on child outcomes; and, four, the potential benefits of external care of children. The issues related to child quality are treated in chapter 4. In this chapter I focus primarily on n, on the dilemmas of childbearing in the first place.

Western civilizations have come to view the family as a sanctuary of privacy and intimacy, a 'haven in a heartless world' wherein outside authorities must not interfere. But since the contemporary family fares poorly on many welfare indicators, the role and aims of family policy are undergoing a fundamental reassessment. Paternalistic approaches will without any doubt fail on legitimacy grounds. In any case, the main issue is not that citizens behave wrongly but that they encounter major obstacles in the pursuit of realizing their preferences. Policies premised on pro-natalist ideologies are, similarly, unlikely to make any major difference. The problem we face is not that citizens have lost their desire for children. The real challenge is to forge policies that enable families to attain their private wishes and, simultaneously, produce public goods.

Families create very important social externalities. Klevmarken (1998) has conservatively cashed out the average monetary value of parenthood at around $22,000–29,000 for Swedish families. This is, in aggregate terms, equivalent to 20% of GDP. We have estimates from the US that the social value of an average child is equivalent to $100,000 on a lifetime basis (Preston, 2004). There is undoubtedly a lot of dispersion around this average. The substantial returns that wonder-kids yield must be held up against the potentially large net cost of the failures. For example, the price of one year's incarceration in the US hovers around $50,000. Poverty is one factor that promotes failures. Recent calculations show that the societal cost of child poverty in the US is equal to 4% of GDP, due mainly to the link between poverty and school outcomes, health and criminality.[1]

Demographic ageing means that there is a growing premium on maximizing fertility. It is also evident that this goal is increasingly difficult to satisfy; parenthood has become more difficult to reconcile with other objectives. To come to grips with contemporary fertility, we need first to recognize the large gap between preferences and reality. From several studies we now know that citizens by and large remain faithful to the two-child norm, stating a preference for 2.2–2.4 children on average in almost all countries (Sleebos, 2003). The distance to actual fertility ranges from substantial to dramatic. In Southern Europe, fertility seems stuck at 1.3 (with some regions at 0.8), and the EU mean is 1.5. The Nordic countries, with France, Ireland, and the UK, occupy the high end of European fertility (about 1.8); the US, with fertility at 2.1, is a rare case of reproduction fertility.[2] If, as is evident in most

---

[1] Testimony by Harry Holzer (Urban Institute) before the House Committee on Ways and Means, 24 January 2007.

[2] The lowest-low fertility syndrome is increasingly also spreading to East Asia and Latin American countries. Barbados' and Cuba's fertility stands at 1.5–1.6, a rate similar to the EU average. Chile's fertility has been dropping steadily in

countries, citizens cannot form the families they aspire towards, we have identified a truly problematic welfare deficit. And if the average family ends up with no more than 1.3 children, our population will shrink dramatically.

Families and Welfare Regimes

We will fail to understand the challenges to the welfare state correctly unless we adopt a *welfare regime approach*. Seen from the perspective of either the citizen or of society, our welfare comes inevitably from the combination of family, market and government inputs. Indeed, for most people throughout most of their lives, the all-dominant source of welfare is derived from the family and market. We receive most of our income from the market and typically most of our social support from family members. From a life-cycle perspective, the welfare *state* only really gains prominence when we are very young or old, or when we fall on bad luck.

These three welfare pillars have reciprocal effects on each other. If the market fails, we will seek recourse in either the family or government. Many basic needs are likely to remain unmet for reasons of market failure, in part due to high prices and, in part, due to information failure – we simply lack the amount of information needed to make enlightened choices. Barr (1998) makes a particularly strong case for the problem of information, arguing that it provides the single best case in favour of a strong welfare state: most sick persons are not equipped to make informed choices regarding the kind of treatment they require or about where to find the best treatment; most parents lack the knowledge needed to select among pedagogical alternatives for their kindergarten-aged children.

The classical examples of both market and information failure are health care and education. As women's revolution matures, demand for child and elderly care inevitably grows. Commercial care services are generally unaffordable to households below the median income. The familial care option that once was dominant is decreasingly realistic simply because the pool of potentially

---

the past decades and stands now at 2.0, slightly below the US level.

available family carers is shrinking rapidly. Family 'failure' is mounting as women's conventional caring role diminishes, and as intergenerational co-residence disappears. Men's rising contribution to home production may have an offsetting effect. But as we have seen in chapter 1, men are unlikely to substitute fully for the decline in female domestic work.

Modern societies therefore face problems of cumulative welfare failure to the extent that neither markets nor families are capable of responding adequately to social needs. Care for the frail elderly is a clear example, since commercial residential services are hugely expensive and because the traditional caring reservoir of non-employed older daughters is disappearing. Where there is double welfare failure, the only logical alternative is the welfare *state*. But except in very few countries, government's role in the provision of family services remains rather marginal at best. Continued adherence to a familialistic policy provokes a growing welfare void that has adverse effects for economic efficiency. As mentioned in chapter 1, women are now generally more educated than men. If women therefore remain locked into familial care obligations, families and society forego a potentially huge source of income.

In its early stages the modern welfare state was everywhere premised on *familialism*. Post-war social policy assumed the male breadwinner–female housewife family and this explains why, until very recently, the welfare state was so biased towards income maintenance and so underdeveloped in terms of social service provision, be it in favour of children or the frail elderly. It was only from the 1970s onwards that the Scandinavian countries – in tandem with the surge in female employment – came to prioritize family services. In North America and the UK, governments chose, instead, to encourage the market alternative, in part via tax deductions. With the possible exception of child care in Belgium and France, the principle of familialism went unchallenged in the majority of European welfare states.

Most advanced societies therefore face intensifying tensions because the female revolution has not been met with a reformed family policy. A paradox of our times is that familialistic social policy is anathema to family formation. The huge drop in fertility and rise in childlessness, in particular among higher educated women across much of Europe, is related to the absence of childcare provision. In parallel fashion, the lack of family services represses female employment, especially among the less educated. Italy and Spain are the clearest representatives of such tensions, combining the worst possible combination of exceptionally low fertility and repressed female employment.

Failure to reconcile motherhood and careers will, for citizens, provoke a trade-off between having children, on one hand, and pursuing employment, autonomy and increasing household income, on the other hand. At the societal level this translates into one of two sub-optimal scenarios: a childless 'low fertility equilibrium' or a 'low income–low employment equilibrium'.

The Policy Challenge

The family remains a cornerstone of society and the challenge is to forge policies that support it. In its increasingly varied manifestations, the family is also key to children's well-being. Hence, as I examine in chapter 4, policy that ensures children against economic deprivation is sine qua non. More generally, the cost of children is rising – and so is the positive externality of children. We need to design an equitable sharing of the costs and benefits of children.

The third upshot is that we need to minimize the penalty of motherhood. This implies a reconciliation of motherhood and careers but we are mistaken if we believe that the standard menu of 'mother friendly' policy will suffice. Some of the major obstacles are hidden in the labour market, especially with regard to job flexibility and security. But policy that addresses this problem will easily provoke new dilemmas. At the end of the day we will almost certainly have to conclude that a positive equilibrium necessitates a 'feminization' of the male life course.

Supporting Families

Demographers use the term 'the second demographic transition' to describe a long-run trend towards fewer births, smaller and also less stable families. Some interpret this as a shift towards post-modern values that prioritize individual self-realization over parenting responsibilities. If the theory is correct we may face a dire future but hardly any policy challenge. Closer scrutiny tells us that the values theory rests on shaky foundations. Take two examples. Sweden's fertility rate behaved like a rollercoaster in the 1980s–1990s, jumping from 1.5 in 1980 to 2.0 in 1990 and then back to 1.6 in the late 1990s. Does this mean that Swedes became, first less, and subsequently more, post-modern? Or if we observe that France's fertility is 1.8 compared to 1.2 in Italy, can we conclude that Italians are 50 per cent more post-modern in outlook?

As noted, citizens throughout Europe continue to uphold the two-child norm. Most surprisingly, there is virtually no variation from Finland to Portugal, from Britain to Greece. While the typical adult expresses a desire for, on average, 2.3 children, there is some tendency for this desire to fall with the age of the respondent. This may either be ascribed to a rise in realism as people mature, or to people's resignation to a fait accompli.

Low fertility will accelerate population ageing, and even minor differences in fertility can have truly dramatic consequences over the long haul – all other factors like, for example, migration, held constant. While a TFR (total fertility rate) at 1.9 produces only a 15% population decline over the century, a TFR of 1.3 will result in a population that is only 25% of its present size (McDonald, 2002). To illustrate, Spain's population will drop to only 10 million. In contrast, the French population will decline to only 85% of its current size. And due simply to differences in fertility, the Spanish old age dependency ratio in 2050 will jump by 138% compared to Sweden's 36% increase. The associated macroeconomic consequences can be non-trivial. Ageing and population decline, it has been forecast, will lower GDP growth in the European Union by 0.7% points a year over the coming decades (Sleebos, 2003).

For policy we need to know what lies behind the child deficit. The conventional theory of fertility stresses two factors: one, the decision to have children depends on the earnings capacity of the (male) breadwinner; two, if women face a large opportunity cost of motherhood in terms of their potential lifetime earnings, they will have fewer children.[3] This offers a credible explanation for why

---

[3] Hotz et al. (1997) present an excellent overview of fertility theory and research.

low-educated and non-active women traditionally had many more children. But the theory comes short in contemporary society. Firstly, cross-national data show that the employment–fertility correlation is now positive. The highest rates of fertility are found in countries with widespread female employment, and vice versa (Ahn and Mira, 2002). Secondly, while in most countries fertility continues to be much higher among the low educated, this is no longer the case in Scandinavia where, in fact, less educated women have the fewest children while fertility peaks in women with university degrees (Esping-Andersen, 2002).

The key to contemporary fertility lies, as all are agreed, in the new role of women and, in particular, in their embrace of a life-long commitment to employment (McDonald, 2002). Careers are not inevitably incompatible with motherhood, as the Nordic countries show. In any case, policy that seeks to boost fertility by inducing women to withdraw from the labour market would be massively counter-productive. As I examine in chapter 4, poverty is hugely problematic for child outcomes, while mothers' employment is not. And considering that child poverty is reduced sharply when mothers work, maternal employment must be considered a plus. It is additionally a plus because financial sustainability in ageing societies will depend greatly on our ability to induce maximum female employment. The good news here is that a growing majority of women insist on having jobs and being economically autonomous.

The quest for children must accordingly be pursued co-jointly with women's new role. Recent advances in fertility research demonstrate that women make their childbearing decisions very differently from the past. To begin with, the male partner's earnings power, once of key importance, is now becoming quite irrelevant. In its place has emerged an array of factors connected to the woman's employment situation. Women hesitate to have children until they have secured a stable foothold in the labour market. The anticipated opportunity costs of motherhood weigh much more heavily, as do the perceived possibilities of reconciling motherhood with their career goals and their insistence on being autonomous.

The opportunity cost or, as it is often termed, the child penalty can be defined as the lifetime income that a woman potentially could have obtained had she not chosen motherhood. The penalty will obviously rise as a function of the number of children and of the total time a mother spends outside the labour force. The penalty combines two components. The first is the forgone wage during maternity interruptions. Measured over the lifetime, this loss is likely to be minor – especially if maternity benefits offer full earnings compensation. The loss can, of course, become substantial if a mother interrupts for a prolonged period. The second, and far more serious, component represents the long-term effect on wages due to human capital depreciation and experience loss caused by work interruptions. Contemporary estimates of the child penalty reveal substantial variation according to type of woman, but also across countries (Waldfogel, 1998; Harkness and Waldfogel, 2003; Rake, 2000; Sigle-Rushton and Waldfogel, 2004).

It is well established that the child penalty rises with mothers' earnings power. Higher educated women, given their steeper lifetime earnings curve, are likely to suffer the highest penalty. But being typically far more career-committed, the highly educated seek to minimize the penalty by having fewer children, minimizing the duration of leave and by postponing fertility. Their superior earnings also permit them to purchase child care (Blau, 2001). Behavioural differences across levels of education explain why, typically, lower educated women end up accepting higher child penalties. As Rake (2000) shows for the UK, the highly educated have reduced the penalty sharply over the past decades while, in contrast, the less educated have prolonged the time outside the labour market. The latter clearly have fewer incentives to return to work.

The behavioural responses of mothers, policies regarding maternity leave and access to affordable child care are decisive for the child penalty. And how these factors combine goes a long way to explain international variations. To exemplify, Sigle-Rushton and Waldfogel (2004), focusing on the median woman, find that the child penalty is especially high in Germany. This is undoubtedly associated with German women's very long interruptions. Beblo and Wolf (2002) show that German mothers suffer a 30 per cent depreciation of their human capital for each year they interrupt. At the other extreme, the child penalty has been found to be minor in Scandinavia. This is ascribed to generous welfare state support for mothers, and to legislation that guarantees that mothers, after maternity leave, can return to their previous jobs (Datta Gupta and Smith, 2002).

American women face, as in Southern Europe, a more hostile environment in terms of reconciliation given the lack of public childcare support. As Waldfogel (1998) shows, women in the US have nonetheless reduced the child penalty sharply over the past decades, primarily by reducing time off during maternity.

As I noted in chapter 1, Scandinavian mothers exhibit identical employment levels to non-mothers. The employment gap linked to motherhood is, elsewhere, rather steep, ranging from a 15% gap in Ireland to 3% in the US. To identify the potential opportunity costs of interruption we should, however, focus on women with pre-school age children. In this case, the Scandinavian gap remains basically zero but widens to a differential of 23% in the UK, 20% in Germany, and 16% in the US (OECD, 2006). To put it differently, most Scandinavian women return to work immediately after parental leave ends. There is clear evidence that the part-time option helps diminish the lifetime income penalty, in particular if mothers subsequently return to full-time schedules (Beblo and Wolf, 2002). In most other nations, a sizeable minority remain outside the labour force for a protracted period of time. These are overwhelmingly less educated women.

Table 3.1 illustrates the magnitudes of the child penalties for Denmark and Spain, two countries that represent opposite ends of the spectrum. In Spain, like in Germany, mothers interrupt far more than in Denmark. The data derive from simulations of the lifetime earnings loss given the average number of months interrupted. The estimates refer to mothers who have two children.

The child penalty that I estimate here is, for Denmark, consistent with what we know from previous studies, namely small. This is even the case among low-educated women who, on average, exit employment for twice as long (20 months) as the average woman. Spanish women take far longer breaks from employment and incur, therefore, lifetime income losses that are four times as large as among other women. We note that the education effect in terms of leave duration is rather small in Spain.

Welfare State Adaptation

Table 3.1 Simulated lifetime income penalties for women with two children in the 1990s

	Average birth interruption (months)	Total lifetime income penalty (in %)
Denmark		
All women	9	5.0
Low educated	20	9.0
Spain		
All women	46	20.0
Low educated	50	21.0

Source: European Community Household Panel © European Communities 1994–2009

Forgone earnings affect in a direct way family income but also the national economy. Pasqua's (2001) simulation study suggests that if Spanish women were to adopt the employment profile of their Danish counterparts, the Spanish GDP would increase by 15% (and government tax revenues by 10–12%). These are certainly not trivial amounts.

As mentioned, the postponement of first births helps minimize the opportunity cost of motherhood. It allows the woman more time to secure her career, and the earnings penalty diminishes. The point here is that birth interruptions incur a far greater lifetime penalty if they take place in the ascendant part of the age-wage curve. Fertility postponement is evident in all countries, but most accentuated in those countries where reconciliation of career and motherhood is most difficult (Gustafsson and Kenjoh, 2004). It is accordingly not surprising that Spain heads the postponement rankings with 31 as the mean age of motherhood.

Delaying motherhood will not by definition result in low fertility if, subsequently, women can catch up. In Denmark and Italy, age at first birth is identical (at 29) and yet Denmark ends up with a 50% higher fertility rate. We do register more childlessness, in particular among highly educated women. But this is not the primary cause of low fertility. Basically the issue boils down to the conditions that favour or disfavour second and higher order births. And, as is well known, the problems of reconciliation are relatively modest for one child but mount decisively with 2-plus children. In North America,

Table 3.2 Childlessness and the probability of having a second child within five years of the first (Kaplan Mayer hazard rate estimation)

	Percentage of women childless at age 40	Probability of 2nd child within 5 years
Denmark	12	38
France	9	42
Germany	15	26
Italy	17	25
Netherlands	20	51
Spain	17	24
UK	17	43

Source: Estimated from ECHP © European Communities 1994–2009

Scandinavia, France and the UK, more than half of all women end up with two or more children; the rate is only 40% in Italy. Table 3.2 highlights the dramatically different catch-up patterns across Europe. It depicts an essentially bi-modal pattern with one group of countries, including Germany and the Mediterranean countries, exhibiting very low probabilities of a second birth.

The main preconditions for catch-up and, hence, for arriving at fertility rates that match preferences are now well documented. Not surprisingly, most attention has centred on child care and maternity leaves. Child care helps minimize interruptions around births and is one major way to reduce opportunity costs. The price of unsubsidized quality child care is inevitably steep, typically around 400–500 euros per month on a full-day basis. This means that lower income families are priced out of the market. It also implies an essentially regressive tax on female labour supply. There is empirical evidence that child care raises fertility (Blau and Robins, 1989; Del Boca, 2002; Aaberge et al., 2005). For Norway, Kravdal (1996) found that a doubling of child care raises the TFR by more than 0.1 point. Knudsen (1999) estimates that universalizing child care in Denmark helped raise the TFR from 1.5 to 1.8. These are substantial effects.

The impact of leave is more ambiguous. If it is too brief, many mothers simply abandon employment for lengthy periods. If it is overly long, the same may ensue (Gauthier and Hatzius, 1997; Billari et al., 2002; Esping-Andersen, 2002; Gornick and

Meyers, 2003; Del Boca, 2003). In the typical EU member state, fully compensated leave is limited to 4 months and, due to often severe shortages of affordable child care, this obviously means that mothers are unable to return to their jobs. And when they do, they are more likely to do so as part-timers.

There is even stronger evidence that child care boosts the employment of mothers. American research finds that lowering the cost of child care produces a 14% increase in married mothers' employment and even stronger effects for single mothers (Blau, 2001).

Towards an Effective Reconciliation Policy
What, then, would constitute the basic ingredients of an effective family friendly policy? To the extent that the monetary cost of children matters, income support via child allowances should be important. As a rule of thumb, each additional child implies a 20% increase in household consumption. There are great differences in welfare state generosity in this regard, with France and the Nordic countries topping the league. In contrast to the Scandinavian principle of an identical benefit for each child, the French allowance is not paid for the first child, while higher order births receive a bonus. The implicit message in Scandinavia is that all children are valued identically. The French approach is implicitly more pro-natalist by assigning a higher value to the third child and no value to the first.

As it turns out, there is very little evidence that income transfers to families with children have any major impact on fertility – with the possible exception of France's third-child premium (Gauthier and Hatzius, 1997). The real justification of child allowances lies elsewhere. In part they do offset the cost of having children and, in part, they constitute a formal recognition that children produce also a collective benefit. If so, redistribution in favour of parents is warranted on equity grounds. If we were to accept this as the primary motive behind family allowances, policy should in principle value all children equally.

The crux of the matter lies in work–family tensions. Gunnar and Alva Myrdal, writing in the 1930s, pioneered our thinking on the issue. They took it for granted that working-class women were compelled to work and their worry was that this would have seriously adverse effects on fertility. Hence, they saw the dilemma as how to ensure that working women would also be able to have children. Today's debate is less pro-natalist, and we would now probably phrase the issue in terms of 'how to ensure that women who want children will not have to sacrifice their careers'.

Since most women now condition births on first having secure and stable employment, high unemployment and job precariousness become major impediments to motherhood. There is strong evidence that fertility suffers when women are on temporary contracts or are unemployed. In contrast, being employed in the public sector raises fertility (Esping-Andersen, 2002). Analysing the data from the European Community Household Panel, I found that women with stable employment contracts were twice as likely to give birth as women on temporary contracts. Public sector jobs typically provide greater security and flexibility and this is why research has found substantially greater fertility among women employed in the welfare state. It also works the other way. Women opt for public sector jobs as a means to minimize uncertainty and maximize reconciliation, even if this implies a wage sacrifice.

Finally the male partner's success as breadwinner may be less crucial for fertility decisions but this does not necessarily imply that men have become irrelevant. One intriguing finding in recent research is that men's contribution to domestic work and, in particular, to child care, becomes salient: women condition births on whether they can count on the husband to help reduce the opportunity cost of motherhood (Cooke, 2004; Brodmann et al., 2007). Women's capacity to persuade the father to substitute depends in large part on their bargaining power in the partnership. The comparably strong position of Scandinavian women favours far greater gender equality in household tasks. Earlier research on Southern Europe found that traditional gender attitudes trumped any bargaining power that mothers might have (Alvarez and Miles, 2003). But as we saw in chapter 1, more recent (and better) data show that 'doing gender' is on the decline, also in Spain. Women's bargaining power is associated with a substantial increase in men's contribution and an even more substantial reduction in her housework and childcare burdens.

Here, then, is one instance of how 'feminization' of men's lives may yield superior welfare outcomes. But it is also evident that 'doing gender' is far more entrenched among low-educated couples. In this case, the choice menu for women with career commitments easily ends up as a zero-sum game with regard to both partnerships and motherhood: they are compelled to either accept major career penalties or to renounce on marriage and children altogether.[4]

If fathers' contribution to home production were, in a true sense, an effective solution to the reconciliation problems that women face, the case in favour of welfare state intervention would be seriously weakened. This is, however, neither a realistic, nor an equitable, scenario. For one, fatherly input to child care or, for that matter, housework, varies hugely by levels of education. Low-educated men remain far more faithful to traditional gender norms (Ferree, 1990; Bianchi et al., 2006). For another, men's dedication to child care is directly and positively related to external care, i.e., fathers contribute more caring hours when, and if, the family has access to paid outside care, or to family carers (Bonke and Esping-Andersen, 2008). The Spanish time-use analyses presented in chapter 1 revealed exactly the same pattern. It is accordingly tempting to conclude that public support is becoming a precondition not only for childbearing but also for greater gender equality.

All told, it would appear that family formation in advanced societies is becoming subject to a set of qualitatively new rules. Women are gaining ground in terms of their command of economic resources and their capacity to exercise autonomy. A comparison between Denmark and Spain is illustrative. Almost all (83%) of Danish couples under age 55 are based on the new two-earner, double career norm. And the average Danish woman contributes 43% to total family income. In Spain, where the female revolution is far more incomplete, dual-earner couples account for only 39% of all and the average woman's income contribution is much lower

---

[4] This feature was also noted by Hakim (2003) in her comparison of British and Spanish women.

(25%).[5] This should result in noticeable differences in women's bargaining power within the household. The tempting conclusion is that women increasingly hesitate to become mothers if traditional gender norms continue to prevail within the family. If so, policies aimed at reducing the child deficit need also to strengthen women's bargaining position within the family. This, interestingly, is where family allowances can be effective. Research shows that their bargaining position improves markedly when public income transfers to families are done in a woman's name and to her personal bank account (Lundberg, Pollak and Wales, 1997).

The standard 'mother-friendly' policy includes a neutral, individual taxation regime, paid maternity-cum-parental leave with job security, and subsidized child care. Joint taxation penalizes wives' earnings and is discriminatory. Access to affordable quality child care is sine qua non for any workable future equilibrium.

It is important to understand that childcare costs are the equivalent of a *regressive tax* on mothers' labour supply. Since high-quality commercial care is priced out of the market for most families, it has a strong social bias because low-income mothers are especially likely to curtail employment – and, yet, it is especially these mothers' earnings that are vital for family welfare. The traditional familiastic solution, i.e., the grandparents, is an increasingly unrealistic alternative because they, too, are likely to be employed. The female revolution coincides closely with the arrival of the baby-boom generation. This generation is now reaching the age of grandparenthood – but under conditions where grandmothers now are likely to have a job. This will have a double effect as far as caring is concerned: a diminishing pool of grandparental help, but also of filial care for their frail elderly kin.

From the European Union's new SHARE data, we are now able to identify pretty well the magnitude of intergenerational caregiving.[6] As is evident in Table 3.3, the frequency (i.e.,

[5] Author's estimations from the European Community Household Panel (2001 wave).
[6] The SHARE surveys, launched by the European Community, are based on a panel design that aims to follow the population as it ages and moves into retirement. One of its most interesting features is its focus on intergenerational relationships.

Table 3.3 The two faces of familialism

	Incidence (%)	Intensity (hrs/week)
Children caring for old parents		
Denmark	20	2.6
France	12	9.3
Italy	12	28.8
Spain	12	16.0
Grandparents caring for grandchildren		
Denmark	60	7.3
France	50	14.3
Italy	44	27.8
Spain	40	25.7

Source: SHARE data

incidence) of interaction and care is everywhere substantial. In a typical European country, half of all grandparents participate in the care of their grandchildren. The frequency is somewhat lower in the other direction, primarily because most elderly parents are able to care for themselves. What comes as a major surprise is that the frequency of caring is *inversely* related to its intensity. In Denmark, where a grandmother is likely to hold a job, the frequency of caring is exceptionally high (60%) but the intensity is low (an average of 7 hours per week). The same goes for filial care of the elderly. Again, the frequency of caring is far higher in Denmark than in the more 'familialistic' countries, but then the intensity is, once again, much lower. Italy represents the other extreme with a lower frequency (40%) of grandparents caring for their grandchildren. But when they do, the volume is close to a normal work schedule (29 hours per week). In Italy and Spain, but to a degree also in France, the continuing shortage of day-care supply, coupled to a severe lack of synchrony between school hours and the normal working day, implies that family caring input becomes highly labour intensive.[7] Perhaps the lower caring frequencies found in Southern Europe capture a reluctance to care at all if one faces the prospect of very heavy burdens. This would imply a logic very similar to that I find for fathers' child-

[7] I would like to thank Marco Albertini for supplying me with these data.

care behaviour: they dedicate more hours when the children are enrolled in day care.

These findings tell us that familialism is far from being extinct. But any realistic assessment will tell us that its effectiveness in reconciling careers and motherhood will decline when, in the years to come, the female revolution nears its completion in the rest of Europe. This means that we must find a model that can guarantee universal *and* high-quality child care. In much of Europe, enrolment of children in the kindergarten ages, 3–6, is fairly high, if not universal. The great challenge lies in care for the under-3s.

Except during the first year of a child's life, which is when mothers are usually on leave, day-care coverage for the under-3s has now become basically universal in Scandinavia. In a second group of countries, including Belgium, the Netherlands and the US, coverage hovers around 30%. In Southern Europe, as well as in Austria and Germany, day-care centres cover less than 10% of the age group (OECD, 2007).

Subsidizing our way to universal coverage does not come cheap, in particular if we aim for quality institutions – which, as I shall discuss in chapter 4, is key to child development. It is well established that market provision of child care, if of quality, exceeds most families' ability to pay. In the US, enrolment rates are surprisingly high considering that virtually all child care is private. Coverage for the under-3s is almost 30%, rising to more than 70% for kindergarten-aged children (OECD, 2007). Such coverage rates are, in large part, achieved through a highly differentiated price structure. Childcare costs amount to $1,000 per year for low-income families, rising to $3,000 for middle-income families (Mayers et al., 2004). The American prices are, however, a problematic guidepost for policy since they basically mirror quality differences. As so much research has shown, only a small proportion of US day care meets minimal quality standards (Blau, 2001; Mocan, 2007). Mocan (1995, 1997) has estimated that it would cost anywhere between US $240 and $320 per child to improve the quality standards of day care from mediocre to good. This would place US prices pretty much on a par with those cited for Europe.

One very important lesson that we can learn from the American experience is that market pricing offers a very imperfect signal of quality. The problem, as Mocan (2007) argues, lies in information failure. Parents lack the information required to make good judgements about standards and this produces adverse selection in childcare markets. For reasons of equity and, equally importantly, of efficiency, a market-driven childcare policy is therefore potentially very sub-optimal. If we adhere to the view that all children should have equal access to child care of similar quality standards and if our goal is to ensure maximum equity, the market model is unlikely to produce any cost savings.

Let us then see what we can learn from government-driven models. Sweden provides what is probably the most generous arrangement, subsidizing 85% of total cost; Denmark is somewhat less generous (66% of total cost) but is demonstrably able to furnish universal coverage, in part because low-income parents go free. The total cost to the exchequer comes to a little less than 2% of GDP, although this includes all ages 0–6. The cost of day care for the under-3s is probably about half that. Public spending on childcare support in Denmark, at US $8,000 per child, exceeds that of any other OECD nation (Norway and Sweden come in second place with roughly US $6,000). This relatively high cost is, in large measure, the consequence of unusually high quality standards across the board: the child-to-personnel ratio is 3:1 for day care; 7:1 for pre-school institutions. The requirement is that staff must have tertiary-level equivalent pedagogical training (OECD, 2007). To put this into perspective, the Norwegian ratio in day care is 8:1; in Spain, where pre-school enrolment is now universal, the child–staff ratio is 25:1.

If our goal were to ensure maximum reconciliation, Danish policy is possibly the best benchmark we can use, considering both sides of the reconciliation coin. On one hand, it demonstrably ensures that all mothers of small children can remain employed. And as discussed earlier, the lifetime income penalty of motherhood in Denmark is minimal precisely because virtually all mothers go back to work following maternity leave. On the other hand, day-care coverage is, indeed, universal. The latest official estimates suggest an enrolment rate of 85% among 1–2-year-old children.

The typical Danish mother will be on leave benefits during the first year of the child's life, and will then return to work – for a brief period on a half-time basis and then resume on a full-time basis. The financial burden on the welfare state may appear rather prohibitive, but it can be shown that the policy is quite cost effective. It is so for two reasons. One, to be examined in chapter 4, is that universal enrolment in high-quality institutions produces a substantial dividend in terms of children's school preparedness and achievements. Two, because the initial cost of child care must be gauged against longer-run dynamics. We know that the lifetime income loss connected with long birth interruptions is huge. As a rule of thumb, a mother who interrupts 5 years to care for small children will, on a lifetime basis, earn 40% less than had she not interrupted. This, of course, also implies much lower lifetime-based tax payments to the exchequer. Relying on calculations for the Danish case, I estimate that mothers who benefit from subsidized child care end up actually repaying (with interest!) the initial subsidy via their superior lifetime earnings and tax payments. If the initial subsidy amounted to 72,850 euros, while the extra tax revenue to government is 110,000 euros, the exchequer has obtained a return equal to 43% (see Table 3.4).

I would like to stress the conservative nature of these estimates. They are premised on a low-wage mother earning only two-thirds of average earnings. Since the per-child cost is identical for all mothers (except for poor households where the parental co-payment is waived), a costing-out exercise for mothers earning average or higher wages would have resulted in a far more favourable scenario as far as government finances are concerned. Many would probably object to this reasoning, arguing that subsidies towards high-income families represent a deadweight cost since they, presumably, would have paid for the very same service out of their own pockets. Such deadweight costs, however large or small they may be, must in any case be gauged against any second-order consequences that might ensue were the rich to opt for private sector care services. One consequence would be that public institutions become ghettos for low-income families. And if, as Mocan (2007) insists, day-care markets are seriously flawed due to information failure, the case in favour of universal public provision ends up very strong.

Subsidizing child care will yield far greater gains if, as I argue in chapter 4, it is also an effective investment in children's learning abilities. There are, accordingly, two major arguments in favour

Table 3.4 Dynamic accounting of the costs and returns from day-care provision

Assumptions:
- mother, at age 30–35, has two kids;
- she does not interrupt employment (except one year maternity);
- her wage is 67% of average wages; and
- she will continue working until age 60.

	Euros
Cost to government	
2 years in creche (x2)	= 24,000
and	
3 years in pre-school (x2)	= 48,850
Total	= 72,850
Gains to mother	
(a) 5 years with full earnings	= 114,300
and	
(b) lifetime wage gain from no interruption	= 200,100
Total	= 314,400
Gains to exchequer	
additional revenue from (a)	= 40,000
and	
additional revenue from (b)	= 70,000
Total	= 110,000
Net return to exchequer	
on original outlay (110,000–72,850)	= 37,150

of welfare *state* support. To the extent that commercial child care constitutes a regressive tax on women's employment, public provision is clearly a precondition for equity and fairness. And to the extent that commercial care can be affordable to most families it will, as in the US, inevitably display major differences in quality and produce adverse social selection. This implies that families' uneven purchasing power translates into uneven childcare quality which, in turn, is likely to produce unequal child outcomes.

Supporting Women's Employment Throughout the Life Course

Where familialism prevails, women are likely to face a major caring burden when they reach mid-life. The probability of having frail elderly parents increases rapidly after age 50. When the caring need becomes intense, reliance on familial solutions is likely to compel the caregiver to curtail her career prematurely. The basis for intergenerational caring is also changing for the worse. Those who will age in the coming decades have far fewer children than previously and this means that the potential family caring reservoir is shrinking. At the same time the size of the at-risk elderly population will grow very rapidly.

As I shall discuss in more detail in chapter 5, the demographics of ageing work against the conventional familialist model, primarily due to progress in life expectancy. Hence, we can expect that the population of 'ultra-aged', i.e., aged 80-plus, will double every twenty years. This implies a potentially very intensive demand for services. Caring for a person with Alzheimer's disease is a full-time commitment.

And we must assume that the vast majority of those women who turn 50 in the coming decades have a strong career preference and will be very reluctant to curtail employment. Higher education was very rare among those women who are now 55-plus, but will be the norm for women in 2020. To illustrate, the percentage of 60-year-old women in the EU with at least upper-secondary level education will double between years 2000 and 2020.

Consider current participation rates among older women (aged 55–64). In Sweden, 65% are still working, compared to only 25% in France and an even lower 16% in Italy. These differences are, of course, not solely due to familial care obligations, but reflect also overall low levels of female employment throughout life. And the official retirement age certainly also matters. In any case, just like we saw with regard to grandparents' care for small children, the prevalence of caring for one's elderly kin is rather similar and widespread throughout Europe. It does seem that Scandinavians care more frequently but then, again, their care is not very intensive. The average Dane dedicates 2½ hours on average per week. The intensity is far greater in France (9 hours per week) and it becomes basically a full-time job in Italy (29 hours per week).[8] In

---

[8] The percentage of older women engaged in full-time care for others is almost 10% in Spain, 2% in the Netherlands, and virtually nil (0.6%) in Denmark (estimated from the ECHP 2001 wave).

Scandinavia virtually no woman need curtail her career in order to care for kin; in Southern Europe it remains the norm (Sarasa, 2005). Exiting the labour force, say at age 50, implies major forgone lifetime income and probably inferior pension entitlements. To society it implies forgone tax revenue.

The rising demand for non-family care cannot be adequately met via commercial care, either in the form of residential care or home help services, simply because both are priced out of the market for the majority of households. A full-time residential place will easily cost the equivalent of median female earnings. For policy considerations Denmark offers, once again, a perfect benchmark considering that care supply meets demand (by law). Here the price tag for full coverage via home help and residential places runs to almost 3 per cent of GDP (home help is fully government financed while patient co-payments defray about a fifth of the residence costs). The model prioritizes home help and seeks to minimize the use of residential care, not only because the elderly prefer the former but also because it is far more cost effective. Even with daily visits, the *per client* cost of home help is less than a third of a residential place. If, on the other hand, there is a shortage of residential places, families will seek recourse in hospitalization which is at least twice as expensive as residencies.

Since entitlements depend solely on need, the Danish model is equitable in terms of access. But need is likely to correlate with social status. This is so because of the huge differences in life expectancy by social class. If, then, high-income earners are likely to be overrepresented as long-term care receivers, equity concerns would point towards a progressive system of financing. On these grounds the Austro-German care model, built into the social insurance framework, will fail to ensure equity. Insurance premiums are levied on a proportional basis (of the wage bill) and are income-capped. This financial system will, considering that life expectancy is socially biased, end up being quite regressive. And the Anglo-Saxon model of means-tested free services to the poor, combined with (tax subsidized) commercial services for the rest, will perhaps ensure some equity on behalf of very low-income citizens but at the expense of major inequities *and* welfare gaps among the rest of the population.

The Danish system is general revenue-financed and this, of course, ensures a modicum of equity that would be further enhanced were client co-payments to be levied progressively as well. Is this model also comparably efficient? It is in the sense of 'clearing the dependency market', but many may flinch at the associated cost. If our aim is to meet demand it is, however, unlikely that the commercial alternative will entail macroeconomic savings, simply due to profits and higher transaction costs. And for most citizens it is anyhow inaccessible unless subsidized. A superior way to gauge costs is to hold them up against the added revenues to government from a boost in older women's employment. If older women remain employed ten years longer than is now typically the norm, household incomes will increase substantially. This means less poverty and need for social assistance and greater tax revenue to the exchequer.

To illustrate the point let us hypothesize that older French women would double their employment rate to Scandinavian levels if France were to adopt a Danish-style care model. This would imply that an additional 35 per cent of French women, aged 50–55, would receive earnings for an additional ten years or so. Even if they were all part-timers, their aggregate tax contributions would probably offset a great part of the full government cost of elderly care. Here we should not forget that old age poverty is especially acute among elderly widowed women, mainly because they traditionally have very little, if any, pension savings. Policies that support women's employment throughout their working life should also help reduce the risks of old age poverty.

Feminizing the Male Life Course?

The female revolution is incomplete also because women's more 'masculine' life-course behaviour has not been paralleled with any thoroughgoing 'feminization' on the part of men. If it occurs at all, fathers' work interruption around child births is little more than symbolic, time-wise the equivalent of being absent from work due to the flu. The only real exception is found in Sweden and Norway where policy provides strong encouragement to take a more prolonged 'papa-leave'. Across their careers, men have changed very little in terms of their employment behaviour, with early retirement being the only notable exception.

When we shift our lens to the way people spend their time, men do appear to have changed in a more substantial way. We have already seen that men's contribution to unpaid domestic work has experienced a leap in the past decade or two, most dramatically in two kinds of activities: in routine activities (such as cleaning) and in child care. In the latter case, fathers' contribution has actually doubled since the 1980s in countries as different as Denmark, France and the US. Spousal specialization in market and home production is on the wane because women are employed and because men contribute more hours to domestic work.

The trend is significant but is not of revolutionary proportions. To begin with, the gender gap in both market and home production remains substantial. Even if women are employed, they work fewer hours, and the rise in males' home production has only produced a modest decrease in women's domestic workload. To illustrate, French men dedicate on average 4 hours per day to their job, compared to 2.3 hours for French women. The picture is exactly the opposite for domestic work: 2.2 hours among men and 4.3 hours among women.[9]

More importantly, the rise in men's contribution is very socially skewed towards higher educated husbands and to families where the wife has strong bargaining power. Not only is the gap in child care between low- and high-educated fathers very large, but it is actually widening. Whatever 'feminization' we can detect across the male life course remains pretty much limited to the upper half of the social pyramid.

Gender symmetry matters increasingly for social behaviour. As already mentioned, there is evidence that fertility among career women depends crucially on whether they can rely on their partner to chip in. There is also evidence that husbands' contribution to household chores diminishes the risk of separation and divorce (Cooke, 2004). Here we may have one explanation for why the

---

[9] These calculations come from the latest Eurostat data (europa.eu.int/comm./eurostat/statistics in focus). The pattern is very similar in the United States (Bianchi, Robinson and Milkie, 2006).

risk of divorce is increasingly concentrated in the lower social strata. Social inequalities in child stimulation are also intensifying, in large part because higher educated men increase their childcare time far more than the less educated. The fact that less educated men seem so reluctant to lessen gender specialization implies that the female revolution appears dualistic, perhaps even polarized.

Marital homogamy is undoubtedly both a cause and consequence of greater gender symmetry. Via assortative mating, women select men that appear more compatible with their life goals. When spouses share similar education or other characteristics, they are more likely to share the same preferences, and the advantages of role specialization also diminish. But, alas, homogamy is not a social leveller. It nurtures more gender equality only at the top, but not at the bottom of society. Women's enhanced bargaining position within the household is a second potentially powerful vehicle for the 'feminization' of men's lives. The problem here is, once again, that educational differences divide the population. Women's earnings capacity is more limited among the low skilled and this group of women is more likely to identify with conventional gender behavioural patterns. In this regard we face a basic Gordian knot that only can be effectively broken by extending the female revolution downwards.

Women's aspirations for economic autonomy and children produce private benefits but also substantial collective value and this underscores the rationale for public policy. The role of the welfare state with regard to parental leave, child care and care for the frail elderly is straightforward and mainly a question of the relative costs and benefits. But if intra-family inequalities are a major roadblock towards a superior equilibrium, what difference can the welfare state make? After all, we are here dealing with an issue that is embedded in the privacy of the family.

Across Europe there is no shortage of symbolic declarations and ideological appeals on behalf of gender equality, but they are unlikely to make much of a difference. The key lies in incentives and constraints so we need to know wherein they lie. The constraints may, first of all, lie in citizens' unwillingness to break with traditional gender norms. But this offers no real explanation since we know that an increasingly large number of couples do actually embrace more gender symmetry. They are predominantly the higher educated, dual-career households where the wife commands substantial economic autonomy. If so, stipulating that welfare state support to families should be in the name (and bank account) of the wife should constitute one promising strategy. A second major factor that impedes employment among low-educated women is the gender pay gap which is, in most countries, far greater for the low skilled than for the highly skilled. The high participation rates among less educated Scandinavian women are undoubtedly related to an internationally very small wage gap. Raising their wages, for example, via a higher minimum wage is a problematic solution since this is likely to produce more unemployment. The major reason why the low-skilled Nordic women find employment – regardless of their relatively high wages – lies in the huge female labour market created within the welfare state – one by-product of its servicing intensity.

But, as the saying goes, it takes two to tango and the principal obstacles are likely to be found on the male side of the equation. What incentives might spur men to 'feminize' their life-course behaviour? Here we must remember that the potential opportunity cost of career interruptions, or of allocating more time to domestic tasks, is marginally greater for men than women, considering that men normally command higher earnings across all education and skill levels. But the reason this is so has, in the first place, its roots in statistical discrimination; that is, employers expect women to interrupt. To compensate for this risk they pay women less than men. If the risk could be neutralized across gender, we would expect greater earnings convergence. In fact, the gender pay gap is smallest in the Nordic countries across *all* skill levels, most probably because Nordic women are exceptionally 'masculinized' in terms of their labour-market behaviour. So here we are back to a different version of the basic Gordian knot problematic.

A popular strategy in recent years has been to encourage fathers to take extended parental leave. By and large the policy has been a failure. We can, however, learn from the two countries where it has proven somewhat more successful, namely Norway and Sweden. From the 1980s to the 1990s, the share of fathers who took parental leave doubled to more than 40%, and the duration of the average leave lengthened. The design of policy made the big difference. First, the leave is not transferable from one partner to the other and this means that the 'papa-month' is lost if the father decides not to use it. Secondly, the benefit was raised to 80% of normal earnings. But if we scrutinize the situation more closely we find that father leave, especially of longer duration, is mainly taken by public sector employees (where the benefit equals 100% of earnings).

Herein lies an important lesson. The career penalty of interruptions is minimal in what we might call 'soft economy' jobs, but this is not the case in the 'hard' economy where competitive pressures can be fierce. The limits to gender equalization via paternity leave may therefore be narrower than we think. A strategy that pursues gender equalization via the men's day-to-day contribution to child care and domestic work may accordingly be more effective across the board. From recent research we know that there are three important ways to stimulate greater male participation. One, as discussed, comes from the wife's relative bargaining strength in the family, and this depends primarily on her earnings power. Another has to do with the sheer volume of work and caring that is required. We can draw very important lessons from our data on intergenerational exchange, namely that the likelihood of giving care in the first place is *inversely* related to its intensity. We see the same logic unfold with regard to fathers' time dedication to their children: it *rises* significantly when the children participate in external day care. If so, a policy of universal early childhood care should contribute importantly to more gender symmetry in family life. The third factor has to do with the length of the standard workday. Within Europe, the Mediterranean countries represent an extreme case since the normal workday extends to 8 or even 9 in the evening. This will de facto prohibit any meaningful male contribution, no matter how gender egalitarian he may be. A reform of working-hour schedules may therefore be relevant.

In any case, we should not forget that women themselves may be active accomplices in the perpetuation of men's conventional behaviour. There is ample evidence that women – again especially the more educated – attach increased importance to motherhood and caring for their children. This emerges clearly in time-use data that show that, despite the steeper opportunity costs involved, mothers are increasing their time with children (Bianchi et al., 2006; Bonke and Esping-Andersen, 2008). The importance that women attach to motherhood is evident elsewhere. As Jensen (2002) demonstrates, Danish women begin to migrate towards public sector jobs in connection with fertility despite the fact that this implies a significant reduction in pay. In a similar vein, Felfe (2008) demonstrates that mothers are prepared to sacrifice wages so as to minimize the kinds of job 'disamenities' they perceive to be negative for their children's well-being.

Men's and women's adaptation patterns may, more generally, reproduce – but in novel form – gender-distinctive life-course patterns. If women actively select themselves into mother friendly jobs so as to better reconcile a lifelong commitment to employment with motherhood, the net result is intensified gender segregation in the labour market: women concentrating in the 'soft economy'; men in the more competitive sectors. Indeed, comparative data systematically show the Nordic countries to be world leaders in occupational sex segregation. The competitive 'hard economy' offers superior pay, but also more insecurity and more intense demands on its employees in terms of effort and performance. This means that the work environment, almost by definition, is not especially conducive to any far-reaching feminization of either everyday life or of the life course.

A New Welfare Mix?

The gist of a new family policy lies in the apparent paradox that family well-being in modern society presupposes 'defamilialization'. This obviously does not imply coercive intrusion in family life. The essence is to give families realistic options. If lack of affordable child care is a major obstacle to fertility, a universal day-care policy enables citizens to form the kind of family they truly desire. There is a widespread belief that externalizing family responsibilities will jeopardize the quality of family life and undermine familial solidarities. All available evidence points towards the exact opposite conclusion. We have seen that intergenerational ties seem stronger and more frequent if the potential caring obligation is manageable, and the same goes for fathers' participation in child care. And a major lesson that the female revolution has taught us is that traditional familialism is now an obstacle to parenthood in the first place.

What, then, should be the relative weight of markets or state in terms of substituting for family welfare production? The debate on privatization frequently pits opponents, who insist that *all* private is bad, against supporters, who maintain that *all* public is bad. The truth lies in the details, not in ideology. The menu of privatization is ample, ranging from a purely commercial regime to quasi-market principles in public provision. In between we find a plethora of options that include non-profit, regulated or subsidized private providers, and voucher schemes.

The first point to hammer down is that, macroeconomically speaking, total welfare costs will probably not change much however we combine markets and state. Denmark and the United States occupy the polar extremes in terms of public social spending but end up virtually identical when we examine total net social outlays (for details, see below, pp. 108–9). If, indeed, markets were truly competitive this should be identifiable in terms of a quality dividend. In some cases, it is demonstrably possible to achieve cost savings via private provision. Home help services staffed by public functionaries will inevitably prove more expensive than if provided by contracted personnel. But in most commercial welfare establishments the per unit service cost will normally exceed the public sector equivalent. This is partially due to the profit margin but mainly to higher transaction costs (such as marketing or billing administration). If commercial welfare providers are pricier, this does not automatically imply that government provision is the only alternative. Both Protestant and Catholic welfare organizations play a massive role in some countries' welfare delivery. In Denmark a third of childcare centres are established and run by parental associations and in Sweden one in ten schools are independent. The real issues we should address are, instead, the distributional and behavioural second-order effects of any given mix.

Unless subsidized (say by tax concessions or by vouchers), commercial social services are typically priced out of the market for most households below the median income. The same goes for private health insurance and retirement plans. A tragic example is health insurance in the US: 40-plus million Americans have no coverage whatsoever. The important point here is that we must *always* measure any potential efficiency dividend against equity. As a rule of thumb, the equity price we pay will almost invariably overshadow any efficiency dividend.

In terms of second-order behavioural effects, there are three kinds that especially merit attention. One kind refers to incentive effects – primarily the incentives to save and to work. Although unambiguous empirical findings are hard to come by, it is a plausible argument that a primarily publicly financed welfare model implies a level of taxation that will distort work incentives and reduce household savings. Vice versa, we should expect more savings and labour supply if citizens need to personally finance their welfare. Until we have credible estimates of the relative savings and labour supply effects of either alternative for *each and every* welfare item, we will be in no position to make an educated choice one way or another.

A second has to do with information failure. Competition may be very positive for quality but many welfare fields involve substantial expertise that citizens are unlikely to possess. Very few are able to choose between competing heart transplant offers and even selecting between alternative schools may pose major difficulties. Mocan (2007) offers a compelling argument for why parents are ill equipped to choose the best childcare arrangement for their children. Clients lack the information needed or they become captive to the sellers' expertise. Citizens' ability to become informed is also highly unevenly distributed. The resourceful may do well in a competitive market but the low educated can be severely disadvantaged. The weak may be additionally disadvantaged if competitive markets lead to client creaming and exclusion. Any rational private insurer would shun high-risk clients.

The third kind refers to social externalities. If a large segment of the population is priced out of welfare services, this may have non-trivial societal repercussions. Take access to child care. If parents are unable to afford quality care, they may respond by placing children in sub-standard care (parked in front of a TV for example) or by withdrawing the mother from employment. The former is undeniably harmful to children. The latter reduces aggregate employment (and tax revenues) and raises child poverty (that necessitates public income transfers). Alternatively, if child care is inaccessible, fertility may suffer.

My argument is that we must factor all such second-order and distributional effects into our accounting practices. And we must compel the advocates and enemies of either preference to furnish us with such a complete kind of social accounting.

The strongest case in favour of privatization is that it enhances freedom of choice and competition; either may raise quality. The weakness of this position is, however, that the implementation of 'quasi-market' principles in public (or publicly regulated) services may yield the same benefits. Greater choice is fully compatible with egalitarian goals if competing providers are properly regulated and consumers adequately informed. Empirical research is replete with good and bad practice from which we can learn a lot. If providers are permitted to cream the best risks or to set fees as they like, the result is very likely welfare segregation. The question boils down to a consistent and effective regulatory framework.

Welfare Regime Accounts

However any country decides to combine public and private, an effective new family policy will require more public expenditure. Table 3.5 presents an overview of the GDP cost of income support and family services. Aspiring towards Scandinavian standards implies an expenditure commitment of roughly 6 per cent of GDP. Considering current pressures on public finances, not least because of ageing, such a commitment would appear prohibitive. Yet, we must not forget that there are three welfare pillars that all represent either direct or indirect GDP use. Failure to increase public spending does not necessarily mean less total GDP expenditure, either because citizens compensate by purchasing commercial alternatives or by relying on unpaid family help (which indirectly has a monetary value).

A basic problem we face is that our social accounting systems are too myopically limited to *public* expenditures. In standard international comparisons we are presented only with gross public social expenditure. Here we routinely see that the Scandinavian countries, Germany and France are extremely heavy spenders (34%

Table 3.5 Public support for families: 2003–2004

	Services to families (%GDP)	Public spending on ECEC (ages 0–6) (%GDP)*	Cash benefits to child families (%GDP)
Denmark	2.5	2.0	1.5
France	1.5	1.0	1.5
Germany	1.0	0.5	1.1
Netherlands	1.0	0.5	0.7
Italy	0.5	0.4	0.6
Sweden	2.0	1.7	1.8
UK	1.0	0.5	1.9
US	0.5	0.5	0.1

*ECEC is early childhood education and care
Source: The OECD Family Database (www.oecd.org/els/social/family/database)

of GDP in Denmark and 30% in France). This seems to compare very unfavourably with the US's low 16% or Britain's 25%.[10]

These numbers are essentially meaningless because they ignore the fact that much spending is taxed back immediately – in particular in big-spending welfare states like the Nordic nations where most public income transfers are taxable. They also ignore hidden expenditures in the form of tax deductions and subsidies for social purposes. Tax subsidies loom large in those welfare models that encourage market provision. When we adjust for taxation and the hidden tax-based subsidies, we arrive at a far more realistic *net* public social spending indicator. And now the massive distance between countries begins to narrow: Denmark's net spending is now only 26% of GDP and France's is 29%, while the US's rises to 17%.

But these figures, too, are rather meaningless because they ignore private market expenditures that, again, are likely to be quite large in ungenerous welfare states. Private (net) social spending is predictably marginal in Scandinavia (only 0.8% of GDP in Denmark) and also in France (2.1% of GDP). And it is substantial in the US (11%) and in Britain (4%). When we factor in private spending, international differences begin to look minor. Total net social spending, public-plus-private, is now 26% in Denmark, 31%

[10] All expenditure data are from the OECD's SOCX database, and refer to 2001.

Table 3.6 Apparent and real social expenditure as a percentage of GDP: 2001

	Denmark	France	USA
Gross *public* social spending	34	33	16
Net *public* social spending	26	29	17
Net *private* social spending	1	2	11
Total *net* social spending	26	31	25

Source: Adema, W. and Ladaique, M., *Net Social Expenditure* (2005 edn.); OECD ELSA Working Paper, 8 (2005: Table 6)

in France, and 25% in the US. Indeed, France is in this accounting procedure the heaviest spender in the entire OECD! I provide an overview in Table 3.6.

One lesson is that some forbiddingly heavy spenders, like Denmark, in reality are quite lean. In other words, the important issue is not so much the overall burden but rather (a) from whose pockets the money is drawn, and (b) what are the welfare outcomes for any given level and mix of expenditure. In Denmark and Sweden almost all the money is taken out of the taxpayer's pocket; in the US, a lot is taken out of the consumer pocket. At the end of the day the average Dane and American end up paying pretty much the same. But what about the non-average Dane and American?

Not all citizens are average and this is where total welfare regime accounting becomes particularly relevant. If a large chunk of the money must come from the consumer pocket, access to welfare will hinge on families' budget constraints. The average American family can, by and large, afford to purchase health insurance and care services but the same items are unattainable for most households below median income. This is why 40-plus million Americans have no health insurance whatsoever, and also why the US exhibits huge quality differentials in child and elderly care.

To cite a similar example, in the late 1990s the Blair government embarked on a massive expansion of day care, establishing 600,000 new places within a few years. The policy was based on commercial centres and, since the public subsidy was modest, families had difficulty accessing the service. As a result, almost half of all were subsequently closed due to 'lack of demand' (Evers et al., 2005).

Increased spending on family services must be considered as a realistic scenario. The very simple point that needs to be driven home is that (a) if we *do* want to realize such welfare goals, this added financial burden is inevitable, however we combine private and public. And (b) if the added spending is not forthcoming we should expect major welfare lacunae, such as lower family income and fewer children.

The added financial burden will inevitably vary across the EU. In countries like Denmark and Sweden a very large slice of the added spending needs has already been effectuated considering that child and elderly care is now virtually universal. The additional outlays that will be required over the coming decades will therefore be limited to population size adjustments or to possible quality improvements. At the other extreme are countries like Italy and Spain where catch-up needs to be huge. In between lie countries like Germany and France where additional spending requirements will be somewhat more modest but nonetheless significant, given large shortfalls in childcare provision and even larger ones in old age care.

In short, we need a consolidated system of accounts that allows us to (a) identify real (and not misleading) public spending, and (b) examine the joint expenditure trends in markets and government alike. It is total GDP use that matters. The really important value of such an approach is that it puts us in a far better position to assess the distributional aspects of our social model. The relevant question is not *whether* we can afford more welfare spending because this will happen anyway. The really relevant question has to do with *who* are the winners and losers, and what may be the second-order consequences, when we opt for one or another public–private mix. If we could also develop a credible system for measuring the implicit cash value of family self-servicing, we would be able to approach a genuine system of welfare regime accounts.

4

Investing in Children and Equalizing Life Chances

The standard critique of the welfare state is that it sacrifices efficiency in its quest for equality. The claim is that welfare guarantees erode the work incentive, reduce our propensity to save and lower productivity. We face a cruel trade-off if, indeed, social protection eats the hand that feeds it.[1]

The trade-off theory rests more on a basic belief than on hard evidence. Serious empirical assessments have generally failed to uncover any serious efficiency losses that can be ascribed to the welfare state.[2] There are equally plausible arguments for why it may actually contribute to a stronger economy. Healthy and well-educated citizens are more productive, and if they feel secure they are more likely to accept rapid change. The globalization of trade and rapid technological change will, almost inevitably, provoke more job insecurity. Many have therefore argued that globalization requires a strong welfare state (Katzenstein, 1984; Garrett, 1998). In a similar vein, it is held that the need for more flexible employment regulation needs to be matched by stronger individual welfare guarantees (Hemerijck, 2002; Kvist, 2002; Schmid, 2008).

The debate has been characterized by considerable confusion, much of which stems from the lack of any succinct definition of the 'equality' side of the trade-off. To arrive at a minimal level of

---

[1] This chapter is a revised and expanded version of G. Esping-Andersen (2007), 'Childhood investments and skill formation', *International Tax and Public Finance*, 15: 14–49.

[2] See Barr (1998), Atkinson (1995) and Atkinson and Viby-Mogensen (1993).

clarity we need at least to distinguish between equality of outcome and equality of opportunity. We also need to recognize that the connection between equality and social policy is ambiguous and often even contradictory.

Equality of outcome is usually measured by comparing the income distribution before and after taxation and welfare spending. There is of course no doubt that welfare states are redistributive, but much of this is simply due to income reallocation over the life cycle, in particular from younger to older ages. It is also clear that large slices of the social budget favour the rich over the poor. This is certainly the case for higher education and the most expensive items in health care. Generally speaking the primary aim of the welfare state was never income redistribution for its own sake but rather to provide insurance and protection. To the extent that the welfare state has ever committed itself to an egalitarian ideal, it has predominantly been to advance equal *opportunities* rather than actual outcomes. In the distant past this was framed in social class terms and the promise was to ensure that class origins should not dictate a person's life chances.

Even the staunchest advocates of the trade-off theory will agree that equal opportunities are important for efficiency, at least to the extent that they are pursued in the spirit of investing in a nation's human capital. To this end, post-war reformers believed that education reforms would, at once, raise productivity and eliminate the vestiges of social inheritance. Towards the end of the twentieth century it became increasingly evident that universal and free education had failed in its mission to equalize life chances. With the accumulation of high-quality comparative research, such as Erikson and Goldthorpe's *The Constant Flux* (1992), we have been forced to conclude that in virtually all advanced countries there has been no significant equalization of opportunities: the link between social origins and children's life chances is basically as strong today as it was in the time of our grandfathers.[3]

---

[3] Comparative research concludes that the Nordic countries may be a sole exception to this 'constant flux' scenario. These countries have, without doubt, succeeded in equalizing educational attainment across the social strata. It is, however, doubtful whether we can ascribe this squarely to education reforms.

A great paradox of our times is the lack of any serious equal opportunities progress despite so much effort invested in the pursuit thereof. As is typical of most paradoxes, they vanish once we arrive at a better understanding of the true mechanisms that guide social life. What is now firmly understood is that education systems, no matter how progressive and egalitarian in design, are institutionally ill equipped to create equality. Pierre Bourdieu (1977) has provided one explanation, namely that the school milieu is inherently biased in favour of a middle-class culture that unintentionally penalizes children from lower social strata. In recent years has emerged an alternative and surely more powerful explanation. Grounded in developmental psychology, the argument is that the crucial cognitive and behavioural foundations for learning are cemented very early in childhood. What occurs in the *pre-school* ages is fundamental for children's ability and motivation to learn when they subsequently embark on formal education. The imprint of social origins is therefore already firmly established before either schools or the welfare state play any major role in our lives. The logical conclusion is that we should centre our attention more on what happens within the family than on education policy.

The quest for more equality of opportunities faces, in many ways, rising obstacles that are inherent in the advancing knowledge economy. In fact, there is a good argument to be made that the knowledge economy alters the nature of the 'equality-efficiency' trade-off.

The New Challenges

The international PISA studies have provoked intense public debate precisely because they provide us with an excellent opportunity to gauge how well prepared we are for the knowledge economy. The gist of these studies is to measure the cognitive skills among youth, aged about 15. Cognitive skills are, in the first place, sine qua non for school success. And virtually by definition they must be central to the knowledge economy insofar as they capture the ability to understand information and solve problems. In many countries, unfortunately, the debate about the PISA results has focused on the national average. The media became obsessed about whether, say, the Germans are really inferior to the French. There are surely country differences but they pale in importance compared to the degree of *dispersion* of skills within any given country. Whether we mainly care about social exclusion or about our future economy, our primary concern should be directed to the size of our population which is de facto dysfunctional.

There are two basic 'efficiency' reasons why we need to ensure minimal inequality of skills and human capital. The first is demographic. Due to prolonged low fertility the coming youth cohorts are, and will continue to be, very small. Over the next decades, the working-age population of the EU will shrink by 50 million. These small cohorts must support a large and rapidly growing elderly population. Hence, we need to invest maximally in the productive potential of contemporary youth in order to guarantee a sustainable welfare state over the decades to come.

The second reason has to do with the rapidly rising skill requirements in the knowledge-intensive economies. While everyone agrees that skills are ever more decisive, there is substantial controversy over what types of skills matter most. Formal educational credentials surely remain crucial. We can, as a rule of thumb, pretty much predict that someone with no more than a lower secondary degree will fare very poorly in tomorrow's labour market. In virtually all advanced economies today, early school leavers suffer three times more unemployment than do those with higher degrees, and they are hugely overrepresented among the long-term unemployed. Viewed in life-course terms, the low educated are unlikely to accumulate much pension wealth and are, accordingly, at risk of old age poverty.

It is, nonetheless, ever more evident that cognitive and non-cognitive skills are gaining in importance. Cognitive skills stipulate how effectively children learn in school but there is also evidence that they remain crucial throughout people's careers. It has, for example, been demonstrated that formal education matters most for a person's initial career moves, while cognitive abilities continue to exert a powerful influence over the entire working life (Warren et al., 2002). The case for non-cognitive skills is being powerfully argued by James Heckman, the economics Nobel prize winner.[4] The core argument is that traits like leadership abilities, communication skills, initiative or the capacity to plan ahead are increasingly decisive for success in modern firms.

Both cognitive and non-cognitive skills are partially transmitted genetically and partially the result of nurturing – that is, of environmental stimulus (Bowles et al., 2001, 2005; Bjorklund et al., 2005). It may be futile to aspire towards an exact differentiation between nature and nurturing effects but there is little doubt that the impact of the latter is very large. Since cognitive (and non-cognitive) abilities influence school success and, subsequently, adults' life chances, the policy challenge is to ensure a strong start for all children. Investing well in our children will yield very large returns both for individuals' life chances and for society at large.

Any serious consideration of equality and efficiency must realize that children are a positive collective good. It is certainly not easy to arrive at any precise estimate of their social value. Preston's (2004) estimate for an average child (on a lifetime basis) of $100,000 may be indicative of the magnitudes. But the question is whether the high social gains that wonder-kids produce are offset by the costs to society of the failures. The Urban Institute estimates, discussed in chapter 3, suggest that child poverty creates social costs equivalent to 4 per cent of GDP in the US. This is in great part caused by the strong link between poverty, school failure and juvenile delinquency.

We might imagine two radically contrasting versions of the knowledge society. The inegalitarian scenario would look like 'islands of excellence in a sea of ignorance', i.e., a knowledge elite surrounded by a large mass of low-skilled populations. I think we can assume that most would favour the alternative scenario of minimal ignorance and a high average. The proportion of today's youth with inadequate skills signals the likely size of tomorrow's social exclusion problem.

I present two telling indicators in Table 4.1: the share of young adults with no more than lower secondary education (ISCED

---

[4] The importance of cognitive abilities is reviewed in Farkas (2003). The case for non-cognitive skills is presented in Heckman and Lochner (2000) and in Carneiro and Heckman (2003).

Table 4.1 A skill profile of tomorrow's workforce in representative OECD countries

	% with only ISCED 1–2 (age 20–24)	PISA (Math) Performance mean score natives	% below PISA minimum	%PISA 'Elite'
Denmark	4	526	5	4
Finland	8	547	7	19
France	14	507	7	4
Germany	15	527	9	5
Spain	31	487	19	4
Sweden	10	518	12	11
UK	8	511	13	16
US*	20	499	18	12

Data source: ISCED data from OECD (2003: Table C5.2). PISA data directly from raw data files. PISA elite refers to the percentage scoring in the top 5th level (in mathematics).
*The US figure refers to those who did not complete high school (12%) plus those who obtained only GED diplomas (8%) (Haveman et al., 2004: Table 4.8).

1–2), and the 'cognitive' performance among 15-year-olds from the 2000 PISA study. Falling below the PISA minimum means that respondents have difficulty in understanding even basic information; this is accordingly a measure of cognitive dysfunction. A quick glance at the table suggests that Denmark and Finland score well on homogeneity while Spain and the US lie closer to the 'islands of excellence' scenario. France and Germany fall between the extremes with an average rate of early school leavers but with a fairly homogeneous distribution of cognitive abilities.

Since it would be silly to argue that some nations are genetically superior to others, these huge country differences, both in school drop-out rates and in the distribution of cognitive abilities, must be ascribed to institutional factors. In principle, Spain should be able to limit school drop-out rates to below 10% and its dysfunctional population to 5%. A striking feature is that the skill dispersion seems unrelated to a country's mean performance. In other words, greater homogeneity need not be achieved at the expense of inferior standards. Finland suggests that polarization can be minimized even when the average performance is record high, and even if a country produces a large 'cognitive elite'.

Another way of capturing the inequalities of cognitive abilities would be to calculate 'cognitive Gini' coefficients. These, again, line up very well with the profile presented in Table 4.1. The US Gini (0.160) is exactly twice as large as the Danish (0.08).[5]

That cognitive abilities matter for labour market success is clear. Using the IALS data, cited above, I estimate that the likelihood of unemployment more than doubles for low-scoring young workers in the UK. In the Netherlands and Scandinavia, countries in which low-skilled jobs are scarcer, the likelihood jumps to four to five times higher than for those with an average cognitive performance. Similarly, when we include information on cognitive test scores in an analysis of wage determination, we find that test scores have, independently of educational attainment, a substantial impact on earnings (Green and Riddell, 2003).

The Mounting Obstacles

Rising Income Inequality

One menace comes from rising income inequality and how it influences the opportunity structure. At one extreme we see top-income households distancing themselves from the middle, in part because of rising returns to skills and, in part, due to concentrations of high-earning dual-career couples at the top of the income pyramid. At the bottom of the pyramid, less educated couples face strong probabilities of low income and joblessness (Katz and Autor, 1999; Gregg and Wadsworth, 2001; Hyslop, 2001). With the notable exception of France, the Gini coefficient of (market) income inequality has risen throughout the advanced societies, in some (like Germany, Sweden, the UK and the US) by more than 20%. Perhaps the single most troubling trend lies in the often substantial rise in child poverty. It has doubled in Italy, Germany and the Netherlands, but has remained fairly stable (at about 8%) in France (Esping-Andersen and Myles, 2008).

As inequality widens, parents' capacity to invest in their children's fortunes will become more unequal (Solon, 1999). This

---

[5] Estimated from the International Adult Literacy Survey (IALS), conducted by Canada Statistics.

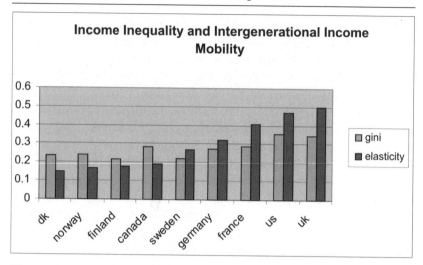

Figure 4.1 Income inequality and intergenerational income elasticities*
*Income inequality is the Gini coefficient for disposable household income in the mid-1990s. Intergenerational mobility is the elasticity of parental income on children's income
Source: Ginis are from Luxembourg Income Study, Key Figures; Parent–child income correlations from Corak (2005)

means that social inheritance is reinforced. This phenomenon has been researched extensively in recent years by estimating the direct link between parents' and offspring's (as adults) income (Corak, 2004, 2005). What we find are truly large differences among countries – differences that are closely related to prevailing income inequalities. As shown in Figure 4.1, the correlation between parents' and children's income is three times stronger in the UK and US than in Denmark and Sweden. France's income distribution is comparatively quite unequal and this spills over to social inheritance. Although not as strong as in the US, the French correlation (0.4) is nonetheless more than twice as strong as the Danish (0.15). Publicly financed education will, of course, help soften the impact of parental income but it will not eradicate it.

The income effect is especially pronounced at the top and the bottom of the income distribution (Couch and Lillard, 2004). As far as the top is concerned, the rich can buy a secure future for even the least gifted offspring. Indeed, here we encounter

substantial over-investment in children that is clearly an ineffi-
cient use of our economic resources. The effect at the bottom is
potentially much more severe. We know from US research that
there is a 42 per cent probability that a child of poor parents will,
as adult, also end up poor (Jantti et al., 2006). Child poverty,
as I noted earlier, has major social costs but it also constitutes a
massive barrier to individual opportunities.

Demographic Challenges
Ongoing change in family structure may also contribute to polarization. To begin with, families are more unstable and the share of
children growing up in lone-mother households is rising. Lone-
mother families now account for 15–20% of all child families in
Northern Europe and the US. The consequences for children's
well-being are decidedly negative in the US, but the evidence
for Europe is more ambiguous. This has undoubtedly something
to do with underlying social selection. In the US (and UK), lone
motherhood and divorce is increasingly concentrated within the
lower social strata, while this is less so in most of Europe. There
are two main reasons why lone-mother families create negative
child outcomes. One is that they are at high risk of poverty. In
the US, half of all lone-mother families are poor, but as we would
expect the risk is lower in Europe: 29% in France, 38% in Germany
and a low of 13% in Sweden (Esping-Andersen and Myles, 2008).
The containment of poverty in Scandinavia is probably less due to
generous welfare state support and more to the fact that virtually
all lone mothers work (in Denmark, 81%). Another reason why
children of lone parents fare poorly lies in the potential 'nurturing deficit' due to less parental time dedication. This, of course, is
especially likely when lone mothers are employed.

A second trend is the increase in marital selection, particularly
with regard to educational homogamy. This is especially pronounced at the top and the bottom of the social ladder so that, at
one end, we see a concentration of two parents with strong human
capital and, at the other end, a concentration of parents with little
education. This should widen inequalities, not only because of
the gap in earnings power, but also due to employment patterns.
As I discussed in chapter 1, in most countries the revolution of

women's roles remains incomplete in the sense that the lifetime career commitment that higher educated women now embrace has not extended to the less educated. When we add to this the far greater probability of male unemployment at the bottom, we see here a major source of polarization. The key lies in the degree to which women's participation is socially skewed. Where, as in Scandinavia, virtually all women work, polarization is muted; where, as in most countries, female employment is concentrated at the top, the gap becomes large. To exemplify, in France women in the top income quintile earn nine times more than women in the bottom quintile, mainly because the latter work very little. In Denmark, top-income women earn only four times as much. Marital homogamy is also likely to polarize parental dedication to their children. As mentioned earlier, there is clear evidence that highly educated mothers *and* fathers dedicate much more time to their children, in particular with regard to what we might call developmental time, that is, active stimulation.

A third demographic challenge comes from large-scale immigration. A curious facet of immigration is that second-generation immigrants tend to converge with local populations in terms of demographic behaviour, such as fertility, but not in terms of education and skills. To illustrate, even in Sweden where the school system is extraordinarily committed to rectifying immigrant children's learning disadvantages, the probability of school failure is nevertheless five times higher for immigrants than for natives.[6] A more general illustration comes from the PISA data which show generally very large gaps in cognitive abilities between native and immigrant youth (see Table 4.2).

In the table I distinguish between raw and adjusted effects. The latter takes into account the possibility that the gap may reflect characteristics that are not strictly related to being immigrant, such as low parental education or family income. But even when we adjust for such factors, the immigrant deficit remains very substantial. In Belgium, Germany and the Netherlands, immigrant children score about 13% lower than native children after

---

[6] This evidence derives from the author's participation in an OECD mission to Sweden in February 2005.

Table 4.2 The immigrant deficit in different countries (difference from country mean)

	Raw immigrant effect	Adjusted immigrant effect
Austria	–60	–36
Belgium	–82	–56
Denmark	–33	–17
Finland	–18	–22
France	–33	–20
Germany	–68	–40
Ireland	+15	+13
Netherlands	–73	–43
Spain	–21	–23
Sweden	–37	–25
UK	–21	–21
US	–35	+14

Data source: PISA 2000 data files. Adjusted effect includes controls for mother education, parental SEI, sex and the number of books in the home

adjusting for such factors. In France, immigrant children score 7% lower. We note, however, that immigrant kids do well – once we correct for compositional effects – in Ireland and the US.

Identifying the Causal Mechanisms Behind Social Inheritance

We now realize that the effort to equalize opportunities through education policy failed because policy makers erroneously believed that the roots of unequal life chances lay in socially skewed access to education. This obviously does not imply that differences in educational design make no difference whatsoever. It is well established that early tracking in schools intensifies social selection, that integrated comprehensive schools do help diminish social class differences in upper-secondary school attendance and that income subsidies for higher education can help boost enrolments of less privileged students (Erikson and Jonsson, 1996; Machin and Vignoles, 2005).

In any case, there is now a general consensus that the really important mechanisms of social inheritance lie buried in the preschool ages. For most children this is also the period where they are most 'privatized', depending almost exclusively on the family milieu. In fact, just about any elementary school teacher can testify to the huge differentials in children's school preparedness already from the very first day of classes. Schools and, more generally, the education system, are inherently poorly equipped to remedy such gaps and we also know from a huge amount of evaluation research that later remedial policies are rather ineffective – and costly as well (Carneiro and Heckman, 2003). This all suggests one crucial point. Whether our aim is to create more equality or simply to raise the productivity of tomorrow's workforce, our analytical lens should be focused on what happens behind the four walls of the family. This is where the really important effects lie buried.

We must distinguish three kinds of family effects: the 'money' effect, the 'time investment' effect, and the 'learning culture' effect. An interesting aspect of these is that they do not necessarily coincide: the rich are not necessarily those who dedicate most time or stimulation to their children; school teachers earn very little, but they read books.

The Importance of Money
The influence of income inequality on life chances is inherently ambiguous. Inequality should, on one hand, create incentives for people to invest in more human capital and, more generally, to be more motivated to get ahead. On the other hand, the prevailing level of inequality in the parental generation will influence parents' capacity to invest in their children. The impact of family origins on children's life chances should be positively associated with the degree of inequality. The standard assumption behind post-war policy was that equalizing access to all levels of the education system (especially via public financing and targeted subsidies) would cancel out the effect of parental resources on human capital acquisition with no need to alter the earnings or income distribution.

Recent research on intergenerational income mobility suggests that this has been an overly optimistic assumption.[7] As discussed earlier, the association between parents' and children's income (as

---

[7] For an overview, see Solon (1999) and Corak (2005).

adults) is exceptionally strong in countries, like the US and the UK, where income inequalities are especially pronounced. We can say nothing about the causal direction between inequality levels and mobility. The twain are bound to reinforce each other in any case. The point is that welfare and efficiency concerns coincide. From an equity perspective, children's life chances should depend less on the lottery of birth than on their own latent abilities. From an efficiency point of view, high parent–child income correlations imply that society is under-investing in a sizeable share of its children (and possibly also over-investing in some).

And we should not forget that the income effect is especially strong at the top and bottom. This is why child poverty warrants special attention. US research concludes that poor children will have two years less schooling than the non-poor. They are also far more likely to suffer from poor health, engage in crime, and fall into unemployment as adults (Mayer, 1997; Duncan and Brooks-Gunn, 1997). Perhaps worst of all, they have a high probability of ending up as poor parents. In other words, the syndrome is perpetuated from one generation to the next. The impact of poverty is perhaps a little less severe in Europe, but this does not mean it matters less (Gregg et al., 1999; Maurin, 2002). For the UK, Gregg et al.'s (1999) data show that financial difficulties during childhood reduce by about a half children's likelihood of advanced vocational training, and poor children are three times less likely to attain higher academic degrees. Their study controls for cognitive test scores at age 7, which means that the effects are independent of abilities. The picture is fairly similar in France. The likelihood of leaving school with no completed degree is four times higher for children from poor as compared to non-poor families (CERC, 2004: 107).[8] Poverty is probably not simply a question of parental spending power. An additional effect comes from income insecurity which produces risk adversity and may lead parents to curtail children's schooling prematurely. In either case, the result is pretty much the same. Hence, if child poverty and parental economic insecurity rise we should expect adverse

---

[8] Unfortunately the French estimates do not control for children's abilities (via, for example, cognitive test scores).

consequences for educational attainment and, further along, for employment and earnings in adulthood.

Poverty is particularly prevalent in lone-mother families. The problematic effects of growing up in lone-mother families have been widely documented for the United States (McLanahan and Sandefur, 1994) and the UK (Gregg et al., 1999). Coleman (1988) reports that US school drop-out rates are 30 per cent higher in these families. While the effects are clear, it is less easy to sort out the precise reasons. Biblarz and Raftery (1999) argue that the adverse effects are mainly related to poor socioeconomic conditions rather than to solo parenthood per se. Gregg et al. (1999) conclude similarly that the negative lone-parent effect disappears when controlling for financial distress. Bernal and Keane (2005), in turn, emphasize negative nurturing and socialization effects.

Most research on lone-mother effects refers to the US and we should be cautious about generalizing to Europe. For one, in the US there is a large overrepresentation of teenage and minority (black) mothers; for another, divorce in the US is more skewed towards low-income couples than in Europe. We should also not forget the very high incarceration rate among young (especially black) American males. In fact, from my own analyses of the PISA data, the strong negative effect of lone motherhood (controlling for immigrant status, socioeconomic status, and mother's education) on children's test scores in the US does not extend to most EU countries. Indeed, the results for countries as different as Denmark, the Netherlands and the UK suggest that children of lone mothers score comparatively better *if* the lone mother is employed. This is almost certainly due to good quality external child care.

If income matters, one would expect welfare state redistribution to have a major effect on opportunities. Government income support to families with children varies tremendously across countries both in scope and generosity. The poverty reduction effect is relatively minor in the US (about 4 percentage points) and very substantial in the Nordic countries (a 13 point reduction in Sweden) and in France (almost 20 points). The pre-redistribution poverty rate is of course exceptionally high in the US, and this means that there remain, post-transfer, 22% child families in poverty. In comparison, post-transfer child poverty in the Nordic countries is, in all cases, below 5%.[9] The merits of redistribution are evident if the aim is to minimize poverty, but will it also equalize opportunities? This depends on the degree to which family income genuinely influences educational attainment. Mayer (1997) presents a sceptical view, arguing that it may have more to do with those characteristics of parents that produce income poverty to begin with. And even if money matters, a redistribution strategy may incur second-order effects such as reduced parental work incentives. As I shall discuss in the final section, the macroeconomic cost of lifting all child families above the poverty line is surprisingly modest, and the impact on labour supply is probably not major. But in terms of cost and poverty-reduction effectiveness there is a much stronger argument in favour of, alternatively, supporting mothers' employment, especially at the low end of the income distribution. The incidence of child poverty falls by a factor of 3–4 when mothers work – in particular in the case of lone mothers (Esping-Andersen, 2002).

The case for anti-poverty redistribution to improve education outcomes is quite strong. Erikson and Jonsson's (1996) examination of the international evidence concludes that the Scandinavian countries' success in diminishing social inheritance over the past decades must be, at least partially, ascribed to their success in curtailing child poverty and ensuring broad economic security within families. If this is so, we arrive at a very important conclusion regarding the welfare state and equality debate, namely that equality of opportunities requires at least some degree of equality of outcomes. The argument that 'here-and-now' equality is irrelevant and that we need only be concerned about opportunities is clearly mistaken.

Still, as I explore below, the efficacy of a redistribution strategy – at least if not accompanied by other measures – is doubtful. Indeed, family income may not be the *most* decisive mechanism that drives child outcomes. A formidable rival lies in the familial learning milieu and also in parents' time dedication.

---

[9] Calculations are from Luxembourg Income Study data. Here and throughout I measure poverty as less than 50% of adjusted median household income. See also Esping-Andersen and Myles (2008).

The Importance of Parental Time Investment

The income advantage that employed parents produce may be cancelled out by a nurturing loss due to less time dedicated to the children. If that were so, children at the bottom end of the social pyramid should be relatively advantaged since labour supply among less educated mothers tends to be far lower. This, however, depends on three other factors. One, on sibling size: with the exception of the Nordic countries, low-educated women have more children. It depends, secondly, on differences in the quality of parent–child interaction and, thirdly, on the quality of external care. There is no doubt that the quality of parental stimulus is powerfully related to the level of education – and of course to 'unobserved' parenting talents. The trend towards increased educational homogamy at the top and bottom may widen the 'quality gap' of nurturing.

This seems, in fact, to be the case. The patterns and intensity of parental time investment are undergoing rather profound – and surprising – changes. Data from several countries show that, on average, total *parenting* time has actually risen since the 1960s. This, as discussed in chapter 1, derives primarily from the surge in fathers' participation. Maternal care experienced a small decline in the 1980s but has seen a recovery in the past decades. Averages are, however, misleading since they obscure widening gaps in parenting (Bianchi et al., 2004, 2006). Among the highly educated – where mothers typically work – we find that fathers' time investment has risen spectacularly in the past decades. In the US and Denmark it has doubled, and in the UK almost tripled (Hook, 2006). We even see an, albeit smaller, increase in highly educated mothers' time dedication. Additionally, the time increase is especially centred on 'developmental' type activities with the children. This suggests that highly educated parents are discounting the value of income or leisure in order to maximize investments in their children. Yet this does not appear to be the case among lower educated parents and, accordingly, we witness a growing social gap on one crucial dimension of children's cognitive and non-cognitive stimulation. And the gap is surely non-trivial. The highly educated parents contribute 20 per cent more developmental time than those with less education (Bonke and Esping-Andersen, 2008).

The impact of mothers' employment on child outcomes is a controversial issue, in particular with regard to the trend towards minimizing career interuptions around births. There is considerable evidence that external care during the child's first year can be harmful. The good news, however, is that mothers' employment *after* the first year has no harmful effects, that is, *if* external care is of good quality and *if* her job conditions are stable and not stressful (Gregg et al., 2005; Ruhm, 2004; Waldfogel, 2002; Mayers et al., 2004). Also from the PISA data we see that mothers' employment (including full-time jobs) has positive rather than negative consequences in most countries.[10]

The Influence of the Family Learning Culture
The quality of parental investment in children is related to the family's 'cultural capital' or learning milieu. This has been shown to have a powerful influence on children's school success (de Graaf, 1998). The learning culture is not simply a by-product of either parents' education or income, and it operates through various channels. One, emphasized by Bourdieu (1977), is the transmission of a proper 'middle-class' cultural baggage – such as self-presentation or language skills – to the children. A second has to do with parents' knowledge and appreciation of education and how this helps them make the best school choices for their offspring. Low-educated parents may have difficulties in navigating their children through the complexities of an education system, especially if they were early school leavers. A third refers to the quality of parental stimulation and, more generally, to parents' ability to actively stimulate their child's learning skills. The international PISA data, once again, help shed light on such effects since they include three indicators of 'culture', among which 'number of books in the home' is by far the strongest in terms of explanatory power.[11]

---

[10] A rider on these findings is needed since it turns out that the mother-employment effect is mainly positive for girls. In a few countries, in fact, her employment appears to affect boys negatively. This may, nonetheless, be countered by the fact that fathers are more likely to care for male children.

[11] One measure taps elite culture such as attending theatres and concerts, but this has virtually no effect on cognitive skills.

My analyses of the PISA data, shown in Table 4.3, suggest that 'cultural capital' overpowers socioeconomic status in accounting for cognitive differences in all countries. Statistically speaking, the 'culture' effect is always highly significant and generally far stronger than income-related effects. To illustrate, I find that children from a family with less than 10 books would enjoy a 9% improvement in their reading comprehension if parents were to arrive at the national average in terms of books in the home.

The magnitude of the 'culture' problem is related to the size of the parental generation that lacks the resources to adequately stimulate their children's learning abilities. In some EU countries – like Spain and Italy – there remain a very large number of adults with only minimal education. Within the typical parenthood age bracket (35–44), 54% of Spanish mothers have no more than compulsory education – compared to only 12% in Sweden (OECD, 2003). The leap in female education will diminish this gap in the decades to come. In Spain, for example, the percentage of women 10 years younger with only obligatory schooling is 13 points lower. But we also face counter-tendencies that emanate from the large waves of generally low-educated immigrants that, in addition, face multiple cultural and educational disadvantages that can seriously jeopardize their children's chances.

Table 4.3 measures children's literacy abilities at age 15. Except for the gender effect, the results would have appeared very similar had I instead used the mathematics test scores. The table confirms the points made earlier. The immigrant effect is strongly negative (and always statistically significant), and mother's employment has, in most cases, a positive impact on children's cognitive abilities. In separate analyses, not shown, I find that the employment effect among lone mothers tends to be especially positive in countries as diverse as Denmark, France, the Netherlands and the UK. Here, of course, we must remember that mothers' employment is measured when the children are teenagers. Parental education has clearly important effects, but primarily via mothers' education. The table displays the unstandardized regression coefficients. Standardizing the coefficients (not shown here) allows us to gauge the relative importance of the family effects. Of particular interest is the fact that, everywhere,

Table 4.3 Family characteristics and literacy scores among 15-year-olds: OLS regressions

	USA	UK	Germany	Spain	Denmark	Norway	Sweden
Constant	425.11***	444.87***	375.85***	452.77***	388.89***	405.21***	433.43***
Gender	18.96***	15.53***	25.58***	15.49***	20.24***	29.69***	27.53***
Immigrant	-16.26*	-14.01**	-40.87***	-19.04**	-25.48***	-35.50***	-35.81***
Father education	3.50	0.76	7.54***	2.32*	8.19***	3.02*	-0.26
Mother education: Secondary	13.80*	10.31	43.58***	19.44***	37.88***	30.62***	20.63*
Mother education: Tertiary	14.58*	15.42*	49.93***	14.12***	52.73***	20.48**	17.16*
Socioeconomic status	1.06***	1.17***	0.90***	0.60***	0.50***	1.01***	1.06***
Cultural capital	33.26***	40.65***	36.40***	39.74***	34.18***	38.78***	30.87***
Mother part-time	16.51**	12.92***	4.96	-17.75***	8.21	4.99	5.21
Mother full-time	-8.15	5.99**	-3.22	-6.03***	-0.78	3.04	7.48
Lone mother	-17.82***	-0.10	1.72	0.36	-0.59	8.57	3.92
R^2	0.189	0.201	0.249	0.227	0.201	0.173	0.172
N	2571	7458	3933	4780	3933	3470	3836

Data source: OECD PISA study

Notes: reference for mothers' education is less than secondary (ISCED 0-2). Reference for mothers' part-time/full-time employment is not employed. To improve upon comparability of education systems, for the United States we include 'some college' (usually two years) with upper secondary education. *=p<0.05; **=<0.01; and ***=p<0.001.

the 'cultural capital' effect is roughly twice as strong as 'socio-economic status'.

If, as I claim, these are the key mechanisms that explain inter-generational social inheritance, we can also see more clearly why ongoing societal trends are worrisome and potentially a source of polarization. We know that income inequalities are widening and that child poverty is rising. The gap in parental time investment is, likewise, growing between the high- and the less educated. Worst of all, there appears to be a strong coincidence between the two, suggesting the possibility of compounding effects.

A Social Investment Strategy

How may policy influence positively on children's life chances? In terms of the 'money' effect, this is perhaps not difficult to envis-age, but can we realistically propose that the welfare state should regulate parenting behaviour?

In a sense, the question is as old as our civilization. Plato was seriously worried about the quality of Athenian soldiers and advo-cated that children of incapable parents should be removed from their family and be raised by the state. The kibbutz ideology was surely more egalitarian with its stipulation that *all* children should be ensured an identical stimulus and, hence, be raised collectively. Such kinds of measures are clearly excluded from any realistic policy menu in the advanced democratic nations. Parents have children because this is their desire, and our societies are founded on the firm principle that the sanctity of the family is inherently inviolable. How, then, might we design a workable equal oppor-tunities strategy?

Reducing the Income Effect

The link between low income and children's life chances suggests the relevance of income redistribution. There are both social and individual costs associated with child poverty. The former are clearly very difficult to assess since the mechanisms are very indi-rect. The Urban Institute study, previously mentioned, focuses on three major macro-level effects: productivity, the costs of crime and the impact on health. The study estimates a total cost equivalent to 4% of GDP, of which 1.3% is attributable to reduced economic output, another 1.3% to crime, and 1.2% to health effects.[12]

Redistribution can be an effective tool for combating child poverty. Yet, we should not forget that family transfers are motivated by other concerns, such as collectively recognizing the positive externalities of parenthood. The seemingly effective poverty reduction we find in France and the Nordic countries comes, of course, at a price. Public spending in favour of families is 3–4% of GDP in the Nordic countries and 2.8% in France, compared to 0.4% in the US and 1.1% in the Netherlands (calculated from OECD's SOC-X data).

At first glance, heavy redistribution does not appear to be a sufficient instrument. France ends up with a post-transfer child poverty rate around 8% despite dedicating resources of Nordic magnitudes. This is to be expected considering that French pre-transfer poverty is about 10 percentage points higher.

An income redistribution strategy would seem attractive for a number of reasons. If the objective were to fully eradicate child poverty (defined as less than 50% of equivalent median income), the price tag is actually surprisingly small. For the US, with record child poverty, I have estimated it to cost only 0.4% of GDP (Esping-Andersen, 2002). This happens to be exactly ten times less than the estimated social costs of US child poverty. But such redistribution would have to be repeated year after year and the *net* benefit should be considered against possible second-order effects (such as reduced parental labour supply). Also, a targeted transfer approach may fail to command broad citizen support, and it clashes with another basic equity principle: if (quality) children produce a sizeable social externality while most of the cost of children is internalized to the parents, an equity calculus would conclude in favour of universal, non-income graduated and fairly generous child and family allowances. If those without children are free-riders, they should be asked to pay.[13]

[12] Testimony by Harry Holzer (Urban Institute) before the US House Committee on Ways and Means, 24 January 2007.

[13] As discussed in chapter 3, Klevmarken (1998) estimates that the value of parenting in Sweden is equivalent to 20% of GDP.

Child benefits should therefore not be confused with anti-poverty policies. If our aim is to minimize or, indeed, eradicate child poverty, we might introduce some form of a guaranteed minimum to families that supplements standard family benefits. If the cost were, say, 0.4% of GDP, we would then need to match this against possible second-order effects. Would parents respond by working less? Would it effectively narrow the school attainment gap of poor kids? As to the latter, there is cause for scepticism since the schooling gap is surely not solely the effect of income but also of unobservable factors, some of which need not be correlated with being poor, and some of which (say, poor health or teenage pregnancy) may provide the explanation of poverty to begin with.

In any case, the burden on income redistribution would be lessened significantly if, through alternative means, maternal employment were to increase within low-income households.

As mentioned, the probability of child poverty drops by a factor of three or even four when mothers are employed. The effect is potentially strongest in lone-parent families. It makes a big difference whether, as in Denmark, the lone-mother activity rate is 81% or, as in the UK, only 35%. Kangas and Ritakallo (1998) provide particularly suggestive evidence in this regard. They simulate what France's poverty rate would be with Scandinavia's transfer system and demographic structure. Considering, as we have seen, that France approximates the Nordic countries in terms of poverty-reduction – but not in terms of post-transfer child poverty – it is not surprising that any serious convergence with Scandinavia's low child poverty would have to come from increments in French mothers' employment rate. But as is well recognized, maternal employment depends crucially on access to affordable child care.

Homogenizing the Learning Milieu

We now realize that truly effective policy needs also to address the family 'culture' effects. But if we exclude any Platonian solution this would, to most, appear to be entirely outside the competence of policy. How, we might ask, can policy induce parents to read with their children or censure television viewing?

One important clue is found in the extensive evaluation research on early childhood intervention that has been conducted in the US. The main – and very systematic – finding is that high-quality intervention on behalf of at-risk pre-school age children has substantial and lasting effects in terms of improved social integration, less delinquency and more schooling (Carneiro and Heckman, 2003; Kamerman et al., 2003; Karoly et al., 2005). The Perry pre-school programme, which emphasizes early intervention with high-quality services targeted at underprivileged children, appears particularly effective in terms of both child outcomes and cost effectiveness. Barnett and Belfield (2006) identify large and persistent effects. Participation in the ABCedarian programme, widely celebrated for its quality, is associated with a 32 per cent drop in high school drop-out risks, and it increases the chance of attending college by a factor of three. Carneiro and Heckman (2003: 165) suggest that through to age 27, it yields a $5.70 return for every dollar spent – in part due to less criminal behaviour and, in part, due to substantially improved learning abilities among the children. Early learning begets better learning later on; a poor start translates into persistently inferior learning abilities.

The logic behind this cost-benefit analysis is very compelling since it incorporates the positive synergy effects (learning begets learning) of early investments into the cost of later ones. The rate of return rises exponentially the younger the child, suggesting that pre-school and early-school investments yield disproportionately high net returns. If the standard monetary rate of return on schooling hovers around 10 per cent, we could anticipate returns on pre-school investments that are possibly more than twice this magnitude. And if the marginal returns are much greater for those who are most likely to fail in school, then early investments should produce a homogenization pay-off, an equal opportunities gain.

Such findings should not be uncritically generalized to Europe where inequalities in child conditions are less extreme. But the crucial point is that early intervention programmes that include strong behavioural and cognitive stimulus can be effective in equalizing outcomes, especially to the advantage of the most at-risk. There is accordingly a very strong case to be made in favour of financing early high-quality child care.

Here again, the experience of the Nordic countries can be of relevance – for good and bad. Denmark and Sweden began in the late 1960s a massive – and very rapid – expansion of pre-school institutions aimed at securing universal access – a goal by and large achieved by the 1980s. The policy was actually not cast in terms of investing in children but rather as an instrument to reconcile motherhood and careers. But in order to cater to the tastes of middle-class families, it ensured that standards were high. As we saw in chapter 3, Denmark boasts a ratio of three children per carer for the under-3s.

Nordic childcare policy learned many lessons along the way. Until the 1990s, for example, children were not eligible if the mother was on maternity leave or in receipt of unemployment compensation. This had the undesirable consequence that many of those children who might benefit the most were excluded, considering the selection effects behind unemployment, inactive status of mothers and high fertility. In recent years, policy makers have tried to make it especially attractive for immigrant and unemployed parents to place their children in public centres. A second lesson was that parental leave and child care needed to be better synchronized. Until the 1990s, the combined maternity/parental leave in Denmark was little more than six months, which meant that a very large percentage of infants were placed in crèches very early.

For these countries we lack systematic impact studies of childcare policy.[14] Indirectly, however, there is evidence to suggest that the arrival of universal pre-school attendance is associated with a significant equalization of school attainment and, one can argue, also with the comparably quite homogeneous performance on PISA (and similar) tests. There is also some more direct evidence. Using the 2003 PISA data, we can compare the cognitive performance of youth who participated more than one year in pre-school education with those who did not participate at all. In the US, participation is associated with a gain of almost 40 points on the literacy test; in most countries, the effect is even larger: a 90-point improvement in Germany, a 60-point gain in the UK.

---

[14] Andersson (1992) provides a rare exception showing that, in Sweden, day care has positive consequences for child development, especially in the case of less privileged families.

Table 4.4 Low-educated father effects: upper-secondary level attainment, controlling for cognitive test scores, sex and immigrant status (log odds ratios)

	USA	UK	Denmark	Norway	Sweden	Germany
Cohort 1	.115***	.185***	.449**	.661*	.320**	.094***
Cohort 2	.097***	.153***	.248***	.447**	.164***	.067***
Cohort 3	.133***	.162***	.213***	.205***	.091***	.098***

Data source: Statistics Canada, IALS, International Adult Literacy Survey Database, Catalogue 89-588, 1996. Cohort 1 was born 1970–75; cohort 2, 1955–64; cohort 3, 1945–54. The cognitive test scores refer to reading comprehension. Reference group for estimations is fathers with ISCED 3 or more. Significance levels: * = 0.5; ** = 0.1; *** = 0.05 or better.

In Table 4.4, I use the IALS data to compare social origin effects on the probability of completing upper-level secondary education across birth cohorts. I concentrate my analyses on children of low-educated fathers. It is vital that we estimate the social origin effect net of children's abilities if we want to capture the essence of social inheritance. Similar to Gregg et al.'s (1999) study, I therefore control for the children's cognitive test scores as well as for sex and immigrant status. The analyses follow three cohorts, the oldest born in the late 1940s and early 1950s; the youngest in the 1970s. And I compare 'social inheritance' trends in the three Nordic countries with Germany, the UK and the US.

The results are very consistent with a *constant flux* scenario in Germany, the UK and the US. In these countries we see no decline whatsoever in the impact of origins on educational attainment across the cohorts – which is to say, over a half-century. In the US, for example, the odds of completing upper secondary education are roughly a tenth (0.115 for the youngest cohort) of those that come from higher educated parents. In contrast, there is a very significant decline in the association in all three Scandinavian countries, and the drop occurs primarily in the youngest cohort – the first to enjoy near-universal participation in child care. To exemplify, the probability of attaining higher education was, for the oldest cohort, a fifth as great as for those whose parents had high education. For the youngest Danish cohort, the relative probability has declined to only a half. Or, if we compare across countries, the Danish youth of low-educated fathers now enjoy an almost five times greater chance of finishing upper secondary education as their American (or German) counterparts.

These results do not, of course, tell us whether equalization was due to child care, income redistribution or, most likely, a combination of both. Unfortunately, the IALS data provide no income information. But the coincidence of timing is very suggestive. It is evident, especially in Denmark and Sweden, that the big leap in equalization is centred in the youngest cohort. This is, in fact, the first cohort in which the majority of children came to be enrolled in pre-school institutions in either country.

The PISA data provide some additional supportive evidence. From these data we can see whether participation in early child care has any effect on children's cognitive test performance at age 15. For most countries such attendance is associated with a major improvement in test scores. To illustrate, in Denmark early childcare enrolment produces a 40-point (or 10 per cent) gain.[15] Additionally, childcare participation diminishes the explanatory importance of socioeconomic origins, of parents' 'cultural capital', of being an immigrant child, and of having a low-educated mother.

If early child care were to compensate for unequal cultural capital, we would expect that the latter's explanatory importance would be systematically weaker in the Nordic countries than elsewhere. The reasoning is that participation in child centres that are of similar quality across the board should, so to speak, help cancel out the stimulus gap that children from low-educated and culturally weak homes suffer. Utilizing once again the PISA data, this is in fact what we find. The influence of parents' 'cultural capital' (and socioeconomic status) is systematically lower in the Scandinavian countries than elsewhere.

High-quality child care and pre-school participation may, accordingly, constitute a truly effective policy in the pursuit of more equal opportunities. Since access to child care is concomi-

---

[15] Pre-school enrolment does not, however, have any statistically significant effect in the UK or the US, perhaps because child care in these countries is of more uneven quality or because of selection effects whereby attendance in quality programmes is biased in favour of already resourceful children.

tantly a precondition for maternal employment – which yields positive income effects – the promotion of child care would appear a perfect win–win policy. We need therefore to examine this nexus in closer detail.

Mothers' Employment and Child Outcomes
The income gain that comes from mothers' employment may be offset by potentially adverse consequences for 'nurturing'. If we take seriously the finding that external care during the child's first year can be harmful, policy would need to ensure a combination of *paid* maternity and parental leave that approaches the one-year duration. In both Denmark and Sweden, leave schemes permit the parents to remain home with the infant over the entire first year – with full earnings' compensation. The norm in most of the EU is no more than 4 months.[16]

Very brief leave arrangements can be doubly problematic. They may push mothers back to work very early. To illustrate, 60% of new Dutch mothers return to work within 6 months of birth (Dutch paid leave is only 4 months), while virtually all Danish mothers return within 10–14 months (Simonsen, 2005). Overly brief leave-taking may also provoke exit from employment. About 25% of Dutch mothers simply disappear from the labour market while the Danish percentage is negligible (Gustafsson and Kenjoh, 2004).

The cost of providing a one-year leave system is substantial. Using Denmark as a benchmark, it equals 0.6% of GDP. This must be held up against the benefits. According to Ruhm's (1998) calculations, paid leave increases female employment rates by 3–4%, and post-leave wages are higher. In part, therefore, the cost of longer leave is recuperated further on via enhanced career

---

[16] Here paid leave implies a benefit that is superior to 50% of earnings. This criterion is important since the opportunity cost of extended leave would become very high for most mothers in the case of replacement levels inferior to this level. If we were to include unpaid leave entitlements and policies that provide substantially lower income replacement, most countries (including the US) would appear more generous, some extremely so. France, for example, permits up to 36 months' parental leave (but at low replacement rates). For an overview, see OECD (2006: Table 1.1).

earnings and tax payments. We should also evaluate the cost in terms of the positive child effects of parental presence during infancy. As discussed, maternal employment during the first year can be harmful for child health and cognitive development. Waldfogel et al. (2002) find that such negative effects are especially accentuated within low-income families.

If we look beyond the first year, the major obstacle to mothers' employment lies in access to child care. As discussed in chapter 3, childcare costs become a *regressive tax* if fees are independent of mothers' (or household) earnings. Tax deductions are commonly used in many nations, but these are unlikely to eliminate the regressive incidence since they are of less relevance for low-income families to begin with.

Kindergarten (age 3-plus) attendance is near-universal in many countries and is often defined as integral to the education system (and thus free of charge). The key question has to do with the under-3s. In large parts of Europe, the conventional solution has been familial care – the grandmother. This option is becoming obsolete because the reservoir of available family carers is in rapid decline. Private childcare markets can thrive, as in the US, because of high price and quality differentiation. But in most of the EU, the market for quality child care is very limited due to high costs. The Nordic countries and, to a lesser degree, Belgium and France subsidize child care for the under-3s. But due to design differences, the outcomes vary substantially. For a standard two-earner couple in France, the cost of one child approaches 25% of their earnings, compared to only 10% in Denmark (Immervol and Barber, 2005). This is surely one explanation for why Danish childcare attendance at age 1 is double the French.

The potential learning impact of early care is also likely to differ. French childcare coverage for the under-3s amounts to approximately 40%. Only half of these children are enrolled in centre-based care, while the other half is placed with individual carers. The Nordic approach (and especially the Danish), in contrast, is premised on high-quality, full-day care with guaranteed access for all children. This requires, unsurprisingly, heavy subsidies: the parental co-payment is only 33% of cost and disappears for lower income parents.

In order to evaluate whether public subsidies for child care are warranted, we need to examine two distinct cost-benefit logics: how child care affects female employment and earnings, and how it affects child outcomes. As to the former, we have clear evidence that childcare availability raises maternal employment levels. A Danish study shows that a 100-euro decrease in childcare costs produces a 0.8% increase in employment (Simonsen, 2005). Since child care allows mothers to return quicker to their jobs, the lifetime income penalty of motherhood is lowered substantially. As I showed in chapter 3, the lifetime income gains and the associated larger tax payments to the exchequer will, over the years, basically defray the initial public subsidy to child care.

The cost-benefit calculus in terms of child outcomes may, in one sense, be unnecessary if child care practically pays its own way due to superior female lifetime earnings. Any positive learning or behavioural effect that it yields comes, so to speak, gratis. In such a context, the evaluation exercise need only examine the marginal learning effects of any improvement in the quality (say teacher–child ratios or pedagogical content) of the system, or of any outreach to needy children (such as those from immigrant origin). The good news here is that the returns to high-quality early childhood programmes are potentially huge. Carneiro and Heckman's (2003) calculation that each $1 yields a $5.60 return may even be overly conservative. More recent estimates suggest a return in excess of $12.00. But again, these estimates refer to underprivileged children who we already know will benefit disproportionately.

Should we therefore favour a targeted rather than Danish-style universal policy? If our primary aim is to level the playing field, a targeted approach would appear the more cost-effective alternative. The choice for or against targeting depends, firstly, on the value we place on equity in the broadest sense. Targeting services to the most underprivileged children can, as US experience shows, narrow the performance gap for those at the very bottom, but unless targeting is very ample it will not necessarily result in overall greater homogeneity of life chances. The US Head Start programme reaches only about 7% of 3 year olds and thus falls far short of reaching the entire at-risk population (we recall that child poverty hovers above 20% and that the share falling below the PISA minimum score is 18%). The remaining 93% of any child cohort will receive care options that to a large extent mirror parents' purchasing power. The huge unevenness of US early care is well documented (Blau, 2001).

More generally, the basic dilemma of targeted policy is how to ensure that it does reach the needy. Here a comparison of the US approach to Britain's Sure Start is of interest. While the former targets problem families, the latter targets high-risk communities. Neither approach can ensure that need is adequately addressed: identifying problem families is only easy when their problems are visible; and in the case of Sure Start it is far from certain that all the needy live in high-risk communities. The real obstacle to effective targeting lies in the multiple mechanisms that produce adverse child outcomes. While income poverty is easily identifiable, this is certainly not the case for parental nurturing practices.

Opting in favour of universal coverage has the great advantage of ensuring that all children, irrespective of origin, come to enjoy similar (high) standards. And if the system helps mix children from different backgrounds, so much the better. US evaluation research shows that disadvantaged children reap very positive effects when mixed with stronger kids (Hanusheck et al., 2003). Yet, the obvious shortcoming of an across-the-board universal model of the Nordic variety is that the most underprivileged children might require additional resources and attention. One example of this problem is the lower participation rate of children from immigrant families. Some form of affirmative action, including perhaps special incentives to target groups, may therefore be called for to accompany a universal approach.

Conclusion: Helping Families to Invest in Their Children

Human capital investments have, over the past half-century, been almost exclusively directed at formal education. It is only quite recently that we have come to realize that the foundations of learning – as well as the chief mainsprings of inequalities – lie buried in the pre-school phase of childhood and that schools are generally ill equipped to remedy a bad start. For policy-making, the learning-begets-learning model takes this insight one important step forward since it helps identify the relative rates of return to skill investments across the early life course of children. It is now evident that investments yield the highest returns in the pre-school stage, 0–6 years, and decline exponentially thereafter. The model is concomitantly relevant for an equal opportunities policy since the returns are especially high for underprivileged children.

All this suggests that we need to re-evaluate human capital policy. As a starter, educational spending in *all* advanced countries goes in exactly the opposite direction from what the learning-begets-learning perspective prescribes. Per student spending rises monotonically from pre-school up to tertiary education.[17] We spend on average twice as much *per student* on tertiary level as on pre-primary education. Moreover, pre-primary spending is, in most countries, concentrated in the ages 3–6. Except for the Nordic countries and, at some distance, Belgium and France, investment in the under-3s is truly marginal.

Concerns about equality of opportunities and future productivity coincide in policies that aim to raise the homogeneity of our human capital reservoir. The share of youth that ends up with insufficient skills is very large in many countries, be it in terms of either formal qualifications or cognitive and non-cognitive abilities. Here is cause for alarm considering that skill requirements continuously grow. Since nation differences cannot be ascribed to genetics, it is evident that policy and institutions matter greatly.

Departing from the dictum that the key mechanisms lie in very early childhood and are prevalently centred in the family, we need to identify how policy can aid families to give their children the best possible chances in life. A core issue lies in the persistence of strong social (as distinct from biological) inheritance mechanisms. Conventional theory has emphasized monetary effects in general and poverty in particular. This is without any doubt a major contributor to differential school success and, more generally, to unequal life chances. But social scientists as well as policy makers

[17] See the OECD's Education Databases for detailed per student expenditure allocations. For tertiary-level spending one should exclude investment in research and development. To be sure, there are needs (chemistry labs, libraries and the like) that inevitably require heavier spending at the higher levels of education.

have paid far less attention to non-economic factors in the intergenerational transmission of disadvantage. Although research is on less than firm ground in this regard, there is a credible case to be made that non-economic mechanisms may be of equal if not greater importance than income. To a degree, the two coincide: teenage mothers, immigrants and low-educated parents are also more likely to be income poor. But we are almost certainly tapping two rather distinct dimensions, and this implies that a strategy based narrowly on income redistribution is unlikely to fully succeed.

The evidence suggests, instead, a two-pronged policy that would appear attractive both from the point of view of cost effectiveness and because it can produce a more equal start for all children. In a nutshell, the strategy condenses into an early childhood care policy. The case for income redistribution towards families with children is certainly evident and requires little additional comment save to stress the point that the burden on redistribution would be eased considerably if mothers were employed. There are multiple reasons why especially less educated women's activity rates are low and access to affordable child care is only one. Nevertheless, if accompanied by adequate maternity leave provisions and with a neutral taxation of spousal earnings, such policy should produce a non-trivial employment gain. And any such gain can produce a double advantage because it helps reduce poverty and, if external child care is of high quality, it may have positive effects on child stimulus. And even if high-quality child care were to have little effect on child outcomes, it is potentially cost efficient in the sense that more female employment together with higher lifetime earnings will enhance the revenue base.

Even if we were to agree that familial 'cultural capital' is crucial, it would appear difficult to conceive of a policy that corrects for differences in parenting quality and dedication. I have tried to pull together what is known about nurturing effects during early childhood. Two factors stand out. Firstly, outside care of infants during the first year can be harmful for later development. Secondly, if external care is of high quality, its effect on children's school outcomes is clearly positive, especially for the less privileged children. What is more, the positive effects persist beyond schooling into adulthood.

Parenting appears to be polarizing. Highly educated parents dedicate more time and effort to their children and the gap is rising. The nurturing gap is primarily due to differences in fathers' dedication which, in turn, has to do with the relative bargaining position of wives. Policy that augments mothers' bargaining power, via income transfers and/or by supporting their employment, should therefore help diminish social differences in child investment.

All told, policy that combines paid leave through the child's first year with affordable high-quality external care should yield important dividends in terms of homogenizing children's school preparedness. A major policy dilemma presents itself with regard to design. Since we know that the returns are exceptionally high for less privileged children, a simple cost-benefit calculus would suggest a targeted approach. What, then, would recommend a broad universal model?

In the first place, one should keep in mind the implicitly dual function of child care: supporting mothers' employment and child socialization. In lieu of the prevailing cost structure, the Danish policy of imposing a considerable but not prohibitive co-payment that diminishes linearly with income is clearly effective (full coverage) and equitable. It may incur deadweight costs at the top of the income distribution, but to Danish policy makers this is regarded as acceptable since, in return, it guarantees broad social inclusion in (and electoral support for) the same comprehensive system. There is also another equity issue at stake. If the positive externality of parenting is substantial, there is a clear case for redistribution in favour of *all* parents alike, rather than redistribution from some parents to others.

This brings us to a second standard argument in favour of universalism, namely that broad citizen support for the policy is considered essential for adequate financing. A third important consideration lies in the high transaction costs and the difficulties of identifying need. Targeting low-income families may be fairly simple to administer but here we must remember that learning deficits are also powerfully related to family 'culture' which is a dimension that is virtually impossible to identify by any public bureaucracy.

At the end of the day, the choice for or against targeting will depend very much on our aspirations regarding skill homogenization. If our aim is limited to 'bringing up the rear' (which is how one might describe US policy in this regard), there is a better case for targeting than if we pursue a more general goal of minimizing, across the board, the impact of (non-biological) inequalities on children's opportunities. The possible shortcoming of a universal approach is that it may not succeed fully in 'bringing up the rear'. Truly disadvantaged children are likely to require an additional effort and this suggests that universal designs may need to be coupled with some form of 'affirmative action' interventions.

What remains to be resolved is the delicate question of reaching those that are hardest to attract and, very possibly, those who would benefit the greatest. Affirmative action policies have a long – and occasionally also successful – tradition in the US, but they would appear foreign to European policy makers. Affirmative action was to a large extent motivated as a means to overcome racial and ethnic discrimination and segregation. This was until recently not an especially urgent question in most EU countries, but now it is rapidly becoming so – not least in light of the visible education and skill gaps we register among large immigrant groups.

There are positive experiences from elsewhere that can help inform our thinking. The Danish government, inspired by US policy, is, with some apparent success, combating immigrant school and childcare segregation by bussing immigrant children to non-immigrant neighbourhood schools. We might also learn from Brazil's previous Cardoso government which introduced monetary incentives to parents to ensure that their children were certifiably present in schools. Even if participation is gratis, immigrant parents are often reluctant to send their children to non-obligatory schooling and this affects negatively their language acquisition and school preparedness. But considering that the marginal value of each additional euro can be very high for a low-income immigrant family, monetary incentives may succeed in raising enrolments.

I think the best way to conclude this chapter is to call upon our elected government representatives to consider how we, in Europe, might implement affirmative action where it is needed.

5

Ageing and Equity

Claims that the welfare state is in a hopeless crisis have come and gone with amazing regularity over the past half-century.[1] In the 1950s many economists were alarmed by its rapid expansion, believing this would harm the economy. Considering the following two decades of unprecedented growth, the diagnosis was clearly wrong. Ten years later the alarm was sounded by the Left which maintained that the welfare state was an utter failure since it had done little to eliminate poverty. But once again, the crisis was overtaken by events: poverty declined noticeably in the 1960s and 1970s, especially because pension reforms provided much more generous income support to the retired elderly. In the 1980s emerged yet another crisis that was even granted official international status via a highly publicized OECD conference bearing the title *The Welfare State in Crisis*. The economists and the neo-liberals had returned once again, claiming that the welfare state was the root cause of high inflation and economic stagnation. Our economies have grown by more than 25 per cent since and inflation has disappeared. Once again, the diagnosis appears a bit wrong.

Twenty years have passed and we face yet another welfare state crisis, this time provoked by demographic change. Projections indicate that population ageing will require additional social spending of such magnitudes that the welfare state becomes unsustainable.

---

[1] An earlier and different version of this chapter, co-authored with John Myles, was published in G. Clark, A. Munnell and M. Orzag (eds), *The Oxford Handbook of Pensions and Retirement Income* (2006: 839–58).

And many fear that ageing will provoke an unmanageable conflict between the generations and that, due to their growing numbers, the old will surely end up victorious.

The Ageing Challenge

Population ageing is, simply put, the consequence of few babies and long lives. Low fertility means that the quota of elderly rises; longevity means that the old become very old. Since low fertility is the prime mover, ageing goes hand in hand with population decline. And if the population declines rapidly this should translate into less aggregate demand and inferior productivity.

The magnitudes can be truly dramatic because seemingly small differences in fertility will have huge long-term consequences. As discussed in chapter 3, a stable fertility rate below 1.3 children per woman – as we see in Southern Europe – will result in a population that is only one-quarter its present size by the end of the century. In this scenario, the Italian population will shrink to only 12 million. France, Britain and the Nordic countries have fertility rates around 1.8, which places them at the high end within Europe. If this level can be maintained, the end-of-century population loss will be limited to only 15%. Europe as a whole has settled into an apparently stable 1.5 fertility rate and we already have a fairly solid prognosis for what this entails for our economy. Both OECD and ECOFIN economists have estimated that the EU economy will suffer a growth-reduction of 0.7% or more per year due simply to our unfavourable demographics.

And why should ageing drive us towards an impending generational clash? The explanation is that the average voter will be older which means that the electorate is increasingly biased in favour of pensioner interests. In fact, average European voters are now already approaching their fifties. When we add to this the fact that older citizens are more likely to be politically active, and that the coming youth cohorts – due to low fertility – are rather small, the political landscape seems hugely staggered in favour of the elderly lobby. We may, as a result, face a zero-sum scenario in which we provide generously for the old and under-invest in children, schools and families.

It is on this backdrop that pension reform has become the central focus in the political battlefield. In just about all countries we find a similar set of protagonists promoting essentially identical solutions. The neo-liberals advocate privatization while the trade unions and pension lobbies insist that the status quo must be preserved at any cost. These positions are neither realistic, nor equitable. The demographics signal that some major reforms must be undertaken rather urgently – also in countries, like France or in Scandinavia, where ageing is slower. And common sense tells us that the reforms we contemplate must, first and foremost, be founded on principles of fairness in order to enjoy legitimacy. A socially just ageing policy needs, firstly, to allocate the cost of ageing equitably between old and young. This point is not especially controversial. But we face a far thornier fairness problem because 'death is not democratic'. The rich live far longer than the poor and this produces huge inequities *within* each retirement generation.

Ageing per se is hardly an historical novelty. Our societies have been getting older and older over the entire past century. But there are three distinct features that are unique to our times. The first is that the process is accelerating rapidly. In the average advanced country the aged population will have doubled by mid-century. The culmination of this process will occur around 2040 when the tail-end of the baby-boom generations has disappeared. At this point more than one quarter of the EU population will be over 65.

The second novel feature is that we have become very healthy, and this translates into big leaps in life expectancy. Since the1960s we have gained more than 10 years of life. Today's average retiree can expect to live until age 80, if male and to 85, if female. So not only will we have more retirees, but they will also consume pensions for many more years. The share of 'ultra-aged' (80-plus) more or less doubles every twenty years and will represent almost 10 per cent of the total population by mid-century. Since this is when frailty and dependency intensify, we face a huge increase in the demand for elderly care.

The third historical novelty is that old age coincides with *retirement*. The norm that we will all retire is firmly ingrained in our social mindset even if it is, in reality, a recent invention. Most workers in the past could not choose to retire, basically because pensions (if they had any) were meagre. If they stopped working it was typically because of disabilities or lay-offs.[2] This is why 'old age' was practically synonymous with poverty as late as the 1960s. All this changed in the past quarter-century. Old age incomes have been rising, retirement ages have been falling, and the complete elimination of old age poverty is a very realistic prospect for most developed nations.

Spending on the elderly will inevitably skyrocket when rapid ageing combines with generous pensions and with early retirement. If we refuse to accept that the well-being of tomorrow's retirees will be inferior to present levels, total retirement expenditure will increase by roughly 50%. The working-age cohorts that must shoulder this additional burden will, we must remember, be small.

In tandem with pension growth we must anticipate a surge in demand for elderly care, not only because the ultra-aged are growing very rapidly but also because the traditional pool of informal family caregivers is disappearing. As a rule of thumb, the aged in general consume 3.2 times more health care than the non-aged, but the ratio rises to 4.1 among those above 75. Complete external care coverage for the frail elderly would cost around 3% of GDP, using Sweden and Denmark as a benchmark. Just to keep up with demographics we should accordingly expect the cost to be more than 6% by 2030–40, assuming steady prices for old age care and assuming steady frailty levels. The former will almost inevitably rise in relative terms because of lagging productivity in care services; the latter may abate in view of improvements in the health of older citizens (Jacobzone, 1999).

All told, we should anticipate an increase in expenditure on the aged of roughly 10% of GDP over the coming decades. The challenge is how to manage this huge increase equitably.

---

[2] Excellent overviews of the emergence of retirement can be found in Kohli et al. (1991), Pallier (2002) and Guillemard (2003). US surveys of new retirees conducted by the Social Security Administration in the 1950s found the vast majority – 90% – had 'retired' because they were laid off by their last employer or due to poor health. Less than 5% reported retiring voluntarily or to enjoy more leisure. By the 1980s, involuntary lay-off and poor health accounted for only 35% of retirees and the majority claimed to have left work voluntarily (Burtless and Quinn, 2001: 384).

Welfare Regimes and the Elderly

The state has become our piggy-bank for old age. Citizens in the advanced countries now naturally assume that the state should have primary responsibility for the welfare of the elderly. In fact, survey research routinely demonstrates that public pension programmes enjoy massive electoral support everywhere. We easily forget, however, that both markets and families remain a central ingredient in the way that the elderly package their welfare.

The family provides services (like care), consumption and also monetary income. Markets furnish work incomes that can be transformed into retirement wealth, and private providers may sell care services and retirement plans. Governments redistribute income and services across the life course and between families. Most retirees receive a mix of all three welfare inputs. Government redistribution is everywhere the dominant pillar in terms of pension incomes (although in some countries private pension plans are quite important).

Today's elderly live very well, economically speaking, not just because pensions are generous but also because most people enjoyed good careers and lives which, in turn, allowed them to accumulate assets and savings. We might say that the labour market was kind to this generation.[3] That was not so for the generations that retired in the post-war decades. They were, indeed, historically unlucky: born at the close of the nineteenth century, they reached adulthood around World War I, began their careers during the Great Inflation which was then followed by the Great Depression and World War II. They could accumulate very little wealth. It is no wonder that aged poverty in the 1960s was massive.

The Two Faces of Familialism

The average old person no longer needs to depend on children for survival. But this does not automatically mean that kinship ties are weakened. In fact, there is evidence to the contrary. Let us explore in more detail how the generations exchange

---

[3] Old age poverty has become marginal, largely limited to citizens – such as widows – who worked little, or not at all, during their lives.

money and caring support. As in chapter 3, we must distinguish between the frequency of interaction and its intensity. Family members see each other more frequently if the intensity of caring needs is modest. This suggests that strongly familialistic welfare models may be counter-productive in terms of nurturing familial solidarity.

Cohabitation with children is an indicator of strong familialism. At one end of the spectrum we find Italy and Spain where roughly 30% of the elderly live with their children. At the other end lies Denmark where the cohabitation of generations is practically extinct. France, with 18%, falls in between. Even when living independently, children certainly do continue to care for their aged and frail parents. Yet familial support is very much a two-way street, and the heaviest traffic is actually from the old to the young.

From research on intergenerational income transfers we know that the flow of money goes mainly from the old to the young. In France, 22% of the elderly give money to their young compared to only 1% who receive money from their children. The net balance is 2,900 euros per year in favour of the young. But family inputs remain, in many countries, the dominant source of caregiving. In the typical continental European country, about two-thirds of all elderly care is given by family members. The Scandinavian countries are unique in terms of universal public coverage of elderly care, and this implies that filial care, while frequent, necessitates few hours. In France, where public care provision is scarcer, 12% of the elderly French receive care from their children and this involves twice as many hours (9 hours per week) on average.[4]

If we face massive cost pressures from ageing, perhaps we should grant markets and families a larger role in the future? One response, favoured by many, is to ease public spending by encouraging private pension savings and by inducing family members (daughters largely) to continue caring for their elderly kin.

The retirement debate is very one-sidedly focused on public finances, and this can produce fallacious conclusions. If it is our

[4] See M. Albertini, M. Kohli and C. Vogel, 'Transfers of time and money among elderly Europeans and their children', Free University of Berlin Research report, no. 76 (July, 2006).

aim to sustain our welfare commitments, shifting the costs to either market transactions or to familial support will not reduce the amount of additional resources that need to be mobilized. The elderly of the future may perhaps absorb less government expenditure, but that does not mean that they will absorb less of the national GDP.

There may be good reasons to reduce government involvement if the alternatives are more attractive and efficient. What we have just seen suggests that dependency on familial care may actually weaken the bonds of kinship. Moreover, increased longevity often implies levels of frailty that require labour-intensive, around-the-clock care. If family members are called upon to furnish heavy caring, it is likely that many will shy away altogether, and this would imply a solidarity loss. When familial caring needs are intensive, some member – usually the daughter – will typically be forced to abandon employment. Familialistic welfare solutions are easily counter-productive in terms of the very same goals they pursue.

There are many advocates of the market alternative. Its importance varies across countries. Private capital savings via employer pensions and individual retirement accounts are marginal in most of Europe, but play a large role in most Anglo-Saxon countries and in the Netherlands. Their significance may increase as citizens respond to the trimming of public sector plans and to new tax incentives that favour private retirement plans.

Privatization may reduce pressures on the exchequer but it is unlikely to alter the future cost scenario. The share of total consumption of the retired will rise irrespective of whether it is financed with public pensions or with investment returns from bonds and equities. In fact, the private alternatives may prove more costly because they inevitably incur far greater transaction costs. And, as Thompson (1998: 44) observes, if private retirement plans were indeed to produce the higher net returns that their advocates promise, the effect would be to *raise* further future retirement spending. And residential care is simply priced out of the market for the majority of families.

One especially problematic aspect of private-funded pensions is that they incur high risks. Firstly, people may live longer than expected. Such plans calculate the contribution-benefit levels on the basis of projected mortality. Since it is very clear that longevity is rising rapidly – indeed more rapidly than was once expected – the consequence may very well be that too many lack adequate insurance to keep them through their entire retirement span. Secondly, company-sponsored private plans can simply disappear if a firm goes bankrupt. The real prospects of mass bankruptcy within the US auto industry would affect the pension savings of hundreds of thousands of American families.

The degree to which the elderly must rely on family support or on markets is undoubtedly a function of government provision – and, of course, vice versa. Still, one does not automatically substitute for another. Family reliance is the last resort when government provision is inadequate and when market alternatives are unaffordable. But we cannot readily assume that aid from kin is always available – not even when legislation makes it obligatory. In Germany, receipt of social assistance benefits is conditional on having no relatives able to offer support. Substantial poverty rates among elderly Germans may suggest that many relatives fail to provide adequately for their needy kin. This is what anyone familiar with social inheritance mechanisms would expect. The children of poor parents are more likely to be poor themselves.

Likewise, market-purchased services are undoubtedly more prominent when government provision is ungenerous but, again, the high entry price implies that they will rarely be perfect substitutes. It is everywhere evident that private pension plans are a realistic option only for the rich. Americans rely much more than elsewhere on private insurance, but its distribution is extremely skewed. Among the top 30%, private pension income accounts for more than half of total retirement income; among the bottom 30%, it is less than 10%. In any case, private pension schemes only thrive when they are subsidized – typically via tax deductions.

At the end of the day, the total *level* of societal resource use for retirement ends up quite convergent among similarly wealthy countries, irrespective of the public–private mix. This we saw in chapter 3 with regard to net welfare expenditure, but it is also visible from data on retirement household incomes. Retirees' disposable income converges almost everywhere around 80–100% of the national average, be it in a generous welfare *state*, like Sweden, or a in a more market-based model, like the US.[5]

It follows that less government and more markets will not much alter the future scenario in terms of *levels* of financing. All it really implies is from which of two pockets we take the money. And here we arrive yet again at the crux of the matter. The welfare mix will not make any big difference for overall costs, but it will affect welfare *distributions*.

There is a relationship, albeit not perfect, between degree of market reliance and old age poverty. As Table 5.1 illustrates, poverty rates are very high in the US and Australia, and the UK falls at the high end of the European poverty rate distribution. The relationship is not perfect for two reasons. First, public pension systems can vary considerably in their distributional impact. Take Italy, where public retirement schemes are unusually generous and where private plans hardly exist at all. Yet, old age poverty is widespread because Italy's basic pension guarantee for citizens with inadequate contribution entitlements is unusually meagre. Second, a prominence of private plans may not produce major inequalities among the elderly if, as in Canada, Denmark and the Netherlands, there exists a basic public pension guarantee that effectively minimizes the risk of poverty.

The welfare mix may also provoke important second-order effects. Strong reliance on familial care will translate into lower female employment and, hence, a narrower tax base. And if women are compelled to interrupt their careers, this will have adverse effects not only on their individual lifetime incomes, but also on household incomes since the income from a second earner is increasingly needed to avert poverty. Since women's employment is key both to long-term financial sustainability and to household welfare, continued reliance on the family also seems directly counter-productive from an efficiency perspective.

---

[5] The relative disposable income of retirees in France is 89% (88% in Sweden and 95% in the US) (Forster and d'Ercole, 2005).

Table 5.1 Poverty rates among the population 65-plus, ca. 2000

<5%	5–9%	10–14%	15–19%	>20%
	Canada			
	Denmark			Ireland
	Finland	Austria		Australia
Sweden	France	Belgium		US
Netherlands	Germany			
	Luxembourg	Italy		
		Norway		
	Switzerland	Spain		
		UK		

Source: LIS Key Figures, Luxembourg Income Study, 2001. The Danish and French data are from the 2001 wave of the European Community Household Panel.

Fairness Between the Generations

How can we identify a stable and equitable intergenerational contract that assures the well-being of the elderly *without* crowding out resources for the young? Again, we need to ensure against adverse second-order effects. If additional financing raises fixed labour costs, for example, the result may be less job creation. The challenge is to define a formula for how to allocate fairly the *additional* costs associated with population ageing. These, as noted above, are likely to approach 10 per cent of GDP over the coming four decades. The important questions to answer are (a) how can we devise an equitable burden sharing? And (b) what happens if we favour one or another kind of public–private mix?

If we prioritize equity, there is a lot to be said for the 'Musgrave rule' of *fixed proportional shares* (Musgrave, 1986; Myles, 2002). To illustrate its relevance, let us imagine two idealized scenarios. In the first, we continue unabated with the conventional PAY-GO, defined benefit pension model. The essence of a PAY-GO model is that current pension outlays are financed from current retirement contributions. In this case, all the additional costs of ageing will, by definition, fall on the working population which, in turn, will necessitate substantially higher employment taxes. To illustrate, in this scenario German contribution rates are projected to rise from 22 to 38 per cent of wages. Imagine now a second scenario where we fix the contribution rate at current levels with no further increments to account for population ageing. In this scenario the additional burden will fall squarely on the retirees themselves. Neither of these two extreme scenarios would ensure equity – and both would inevitably be accompanied by very negative second-order effects. In other words, neither is likely to constitute a viable and fair generational contract.

Let us think of the problem from the point of view of generations. How might a three-generation family, committed to risk sharing, resolve the dilemma? If citizens are content with the status quo (they are happy with the relative levels of consumption of the generations that now obtain), they would undoubtedly opt for a fixed relative position (FRP) model akin to that advocated by Musgrave (1986).[6] Contributions and benefits are set so as to hold *constant* the ratio of per capita earnings of those in the working population (net of contributions) to the per capita benefits (net of taxes) of retirees. Once the ratio is fixed, the tax rate is adjusted periodically to reflect both population and productivity changes. As the population ages, the tax rate rises but benefits also fall so that both parties 'lose' at the same rate (i.e., both net earnings and benefits rise more slowly than they would in the absence of population ageing). Simply put, the Musgrave rule helps allocate the additional burden equitably between the generations. Its starting point is to fix proportionally the per capita incomes of workers and retirees. Any additional expenditure would, according to the rule, be allocated proportionally.

If we shift our perspective from a 'point-in-time' to a life-course framework, the case for Musgrave's solution is even more persuasive. What are the implications of the three alternative pension models for the *entire* life course of cohorts born today and in the future? What will be the legacy that we leave to our children and grandchildren?

---

[6] The FRP principle, however, would not satisfy a concept of fairness defined by the notion that each generation ought to pay the same proportion of salary to get the same level of pension rights during retirement. On a three-generational 'family farm', for example, the *share* of output required to support ageing parents in retirement under FRP will be larger when there are two producers in the working-age generation than when there are four.

Under existing PAY-GO defined benefit rules, future cohorts will experience declining living standards in childhood and during their working years, but then they will enjoy a relatively affluent old age. If contribution rates are fixed, now the strategy in several countries, future generations will enjoy prosperous childhoods and working lives but relative penury in old age. The Musgrave strategy, in contrast, effectively smoothes the change across the entire life course and maintains the status quo with respect to the lifetime distribution of income. In this respect it is a 'conservative' strategy based on the assumption that, on average, the lifetime distribution of income available to current generations should be preserved more or less intact into the future. Future generations may of course disagree with our judgements and conclude they want a different allocation of income over the life course. The point to note here is that if it is possible to agree on a fair proportionality, the future financial scenario will be stable and will also be perceived as intergenerationally fair.

But only up to a point. First, the Musgrave rule is easy to apply to a government-dominated pension regime, but encounters obstacles where private schemes proliferate. Indeed, the equity pursued in the public pension domain may very easily become undone in the private domain. In brief, the strategy requires that private plans be co-integrated into an overall accounting scheme. The often very favourable tax treatment of private schemes clearly warrants that they, too, be charged with social responsibility.

Second, the Musgrave principle will remain equitable only if relative prices in the consumer basket of the young and old also remain stable. This is where the future of pensions and health come together. If health and caring services are prone to price inflation, the intergenerational 'pension' contract will be in jeopardy. Indeed, if so, there is a case to be made that intergenerational equity will require that the elderly receive a larger per capita share of national income.[7] This is all the more so since we know that pension incomes decline with age. In other words, when care services are most needed is exactly when retirees least can afford them.

---

[7] This point was first raised by Frank Vandenbroucke (2002).

Third, the Musgrave rule is limited to intergenerational equity and ignores the much larger problems of inequality *within* generations. As Wolfson et al. (1998) demonstrate, the enormous inequalities within any generation dwarf the differences between generations in the distribution of 'winners' and 'losers'. Indeed, it is possible that policies in favour of intergenerational equity may exacerbate intragenerational inequities. To illustrate this, let us examine the possible ramifications of postponing retirement age, on one hand, and on pension financing, on the other hand.

Working Longer

Until recently, the lifespan of a typical male citizen was completely dominated by work. Four decades ago he would dedicate about 8 years to education, 45 years to employment and perhaps 5 or, with luck, 10 years to retirement. All in all, the non-work part of his life was less than half that of his work part. Today we study and live longer and we move into retirement much earlier. In a typical EU country, the average number of school years is now 11, and the average male has added 8 or 10 years to his life expectancy. The result is that the number of working years has dropped to less than 40 which is now also the number of years that a typical male spends not working.

Most now agree that by far the most effective policy is to delay the age of retirement. Considering postponed entry into employment and gains in longevity, such a strategy is entirely consistent with the Musgrave rule: it seems fair in intergenerational terms. The OECD (2001: 69) estimates that a ten-month postponement is financially equivalent to a 10 per cent cut in pension benefits. The Danish government's recent Welfare Commission estimates that a one month per year increase in retirement age over the coming three decades (equivalent to a little less than 3 years in total) would ensure financial sustainability at present welfare levels. Generally speaking, a return to age 65 as the norm would probably come close to 'balancing the books'. To illustrate, simulations undertaken by the OECD show that a five-year postponement of retirement in France would reduce the old age dependency ratio from 0.7 to 0.5 by mid-century. Delaying retirement is a very effective tool because it cuts both ways:

reducing pension years while simultaneously raising contribution years.

Delaying retirement may, however, produce intragenerational injustice. Here we return to the inequalities of death. In France, an average professional male will live 5 years longer than a manual worker.[8] Just as an additional year of retirement represents a larger proportional gain for someone with a 7-year life expectancy than for someone with a 12-year life expectancy, an additional year of employment represents a proportionately greater loss for those with shorter life expectancies. Since health, life expectancy, disability and wealth are all strongly correlated, the equity problem is compounded. Moreover, the recent gains in longevity have gone disproportionately to the most affluent (Hattersley, 1999), thus reinforcing the association. If the 'rich' are the main consumers of future high-cost items, such as pensions, health and long-term care, we would need to tax citizens more progressively according to their life expectancy.[9]

Equitable Financing

Today's pay-as-you-go pensions are financed with a payroll tax while income from capital and transfers (including pension income) are exempt.[10] The payroll tax is a flat tax, often with a wage ceiling that makes it regressive. There are typically no exemptions and no allowances for family size. In effect, charging the additional costs of ageing to payroll taxes creates a huge problem of equity within the working-age population since the distribution of the additional costs in no way reflects ability to pay.

We therefore face the formidable challenge of defining allocation rules that are also intragenerationally equitable among the retired

[8] See Cambois et al. (2001: Table 3). The gap is even wider (about 7 years, and worsening) in Britain according to Wilkinson (forthcoming).

[9] The probability of survival is substantially higher among the rich, but so also is their expectancy of disability-free years. At the age of 60, French managers can expect four more disability-free years than a manual worker. Also, it is worth noting that the 'disability gap' between the two groups is widening over time (Cambois et al., 2001: Table 5).

[10] For purposes of this discussion, I adopt the standard assumption that payroll taxes, even when borne by the employer, are additions to labour costs that are ultimately borne by employees, typically in the form of lower wages.

as well as the working population. If the cost of being old rises disproportionally among those with low incomes, then a Musgrave-type fixed proportions rule will end up being unfair. If, moreover, the rich consume more pensions, health or care services then, once again, a purely *inter*generational contract will result in unfairness.

To ensure equitable burden-sharing, one would clearly need to undertake major revisions of tax and contribution schedules, not only in terms of raising the progressiveness of public revenues targeted at the aged, but also of diminishing the regressive nature of tax subsidies that benefit private retirement plans.

If we take a longer perspective, both the future financial burden and its associated distributional consequences will depend very much on the kinds of lives that the coming cohorts will have. If we begin to reform pension systems today, this will probably not affect today's elderly. Those most affected will be our children and grandchildren. At mid-century, those who are now children will approach retirement. The real challenge we face is to realistically project how these new generations will fare in the coming half-century. Happily, we can rely on more than fortune-tellers and crystal balls.

Pension Reform with Our Children in Mind: Beyond the Generational Contract

A secure retirement depends very much on how we fared during our working lives and this, in turn, correlates powerfully with the quality of our childhood and youth. The retirement prospects for our children and grandchildren 40 or 50 years from now, as well as their ability to finance *our* retirement and care needs until then, are similarly contingent on the kinds of lives they will have. In short, securing retirement for the year 2040 or 2050 depends more on the quality, quantity and *distribution* of the stock of productive assets – physical, human and environmental – that our children inherit than on any reforms we now introduce to the design of our pension systems.

To illustrate, consider the retirement prospects of the cohorts likely to retire in 2040. They turned 30 in 2005, old enough for us to discern who will and who won't be well placed to provide themselves with a secure retirement. The welfare state edifice that we know today was created in response to a profile of risks and needs that prevailed in the age of our grandparents, parents and those of us who came to maturity in the post-war decades. Today's young workers face a very different risk profile, and this needs to be factored into our retirement projections for mid-century.

The Changing Life Course and New Inequalities

In a 1944 League of Nations report on post-war labour needs, a group of Princeton demographers worried about the economic impact of population ageing because they assumed that, in 'industrial societies', maximum productivity is reached by age 35 (Notestein et al., 1944). The success of industrial economies depended, in their view, on large numbers of muscular young men. As I pointed out in chapter 1, the age of leaving the parental home, marriage and childbirth – markers of achieving economic independence – all fell to a historical minimum in the post-war decades. All this suggested that industrial economies did indeed place a high economic value on young workers (Beaujot, 2004; Corijn and Klijzing, 2001). The contemporary cohorts of retirees reached social and economic maturity relatively early in the life course.

All this has changed, with dramatic implications for the types of careers and family life that today's young will experience as they progress towards their retirement years. Indeed, the revolution in life-course patterns of young adults in the past 40 years is as much a part of the phenomenon of 'population ageing' as is the much-vaunted arrival of the baby boom. Postponed independence, longer education and later union formation lead to lower levels of childbearing.

As with any major change there is good news for some and bad news for others. Starting later means fewer years in the labour market with less opportunity to save or earn benefits early in the life course. Future cohorts may therefore need to postpone retirement. However, starting late has always been the case among the highly educated. Retirement decisions clearly depend on other factors.

First, while total hours and years worked by individuals have fallen, this is not the case for families since women's labour supply has grown sharply. The rise in 'family' years and hours worked helps pay for more years of retirement (Burtless and Quinn, 2001). This implies that stable two-income couples will arrive at age 65 well positioned to enjoy a secure retirement while single-earner households and the rising number of never-married and divorced will face greater risks of poverty in old age. The latter group has become very large in modern societies.

The increase in marital homogamy is a possible source of growing polarization. The well educated tend to marry one another, forming families with high earnings and few risks of unemployment. Their marriages are also more stable. Less educated couples have lower wages and are far more likely to experience periods without work. Additionally, lower educated women are far less likely to be employed. And divorce as well as lone motherhood is far more likely among the less educated. The upshot is that the gap in family income and in expected retirement income between the top and bottom widens.

This is illustrated by recent estimates for the US. In 2000, the incomes among top-quintile retirees are eight times those of the bottom quintile; this will rise to ten times when the baby boomers retire – simply as a result of greater earnings' inequality. Among current US retirees, the income of high school drop-outs is 68% of the mean of their age cohort. The rising earnings gap means this figure will fall to 53% when the baby boomers retire (Butrica, Iams and Smith, 2003).

It is virtually certain, then, that the stable, dual-earner, university educated couple of today will be able to retire in relative affluence in 2040 *irrespective* of what happens to national pension systems. And well-educated childless couples will be the best positioned of all. The fate of low-educated couples is bleak. They have, of course, potentially more working years but they face substantial risks of unemployment and low earnings, all of which will affect their subsequent retirement resources.

There are two paradoxes associated with this scenario. First, we would reap the largest economic gains if the most productive workers remain in employment longer; yet they are the very people who will be the best positioned to retire early. High-income earners have substantial retirement savings and are therefore more immune to any policies designed to postpone retirement.

Second, as we have noted, it is the well educated whose retirement will cost the most simply because their life expectancy is far longer. They will consume a larger share of the national retirement budget and incur the larger health and care costs that arise as a result of increasing frailty at advanced old age. And the childless will require the most assistance of all.

Since, by definition and design, old age *insurance* transfers income from those with shorter to those with greater life expectancy, these two features raise important questions of *intragenerational* distributive justice.

As the knowledge intensity of our economies increases, citizens with low education and insufficient cognitive skills will, with growing likelihood, find themselves locked into a life of low wages and precarious employment. A problematic working life in the coming decades will raise the likelihood of poverty in old age to a greater degree than among today's retirees. As I examined in chapter 4, we can with some certainty predict the size of this high-risk population over the next decades simply by looking at data on early school leavers among today's youth. For the EU as a whole, a fifth of contemporary youth faces the real probability of old age poverty at mid-century.

Future inequalities are fuelled additionally by the new demographics. The size of children's inheritance depends of course on their parents' wealth, but also on the number of siblings that must share it. Low fertility means that each child will receive more. But since fertility is inversely related to education and income, inequalities due to social inheritance are likely to be far greater. Since well-off parents have fewer children, they can invest far greater resources *per child* during childhood and youth and later they will leave disproportionately greater *per child* bequests.

Retirement Reform must Begin with Babies

Securing retirement for mid-century will depend as much on the quality, quantity and allocation of our productive assets as on any reforms we make now to the design of our pension systems. Higher productivity will help us to pay the additional costs of population ageing but it will not solve the associated distributional issues. And we know that high-productivity economies are not necessarily the most equitable in distributional terms.

Paradoxically, then, there is a sound argument that good retirement policy must begin with babies. The distribution of welfare among tomorrow's retirees will above all hinge on the inequalities in life chances among today's children. If policy makers are seriously concerned about equitable retirement in the future, the obvious first step would be to ensure more equality now of cognitive stimulation and educational attainment in childhood.

Our legacy to the next generation also includes the real welfare gains embedded in our social institutions, including those that enable the young to care for the old. The traditional family structure in which parents care for children when they are too young to work and children support their parents when they are old and frail are important characteristics of the human species, probably with deep biological roots. This seems quite evident when we recall that Danes care for their frail elderly with unusual frequency despite the fact that their welfare state furnishes de facto complete external care support. Contemporary historiography confirms that the emergence of mandatory public pensions was as important for the young as for the old, a form of risk-sharing not only against the risk of one's *own* longevity but also against the risk of *one's parents'* longevity and the imperative of supporting parents financially through an extended old age. For a species motivated by 'filial piety', old age security is also welfare policy for the young. Rising pension costs may lead our children to complain about high taxes. It is unlikely, however, that they will be grateful if they must support us directly to the age of 95. Just as intergenerational justice requires us to leave them with a sustainable environment, it also requires us to leave them with institutions at least as good as those we have had to care for our parents in their old age.

If this is our bottom-line criterion for policy, how then might an 'at least as good' institutional environment be assured? As far as pension reform is concerned, most experts agree on a set of core fundamentals. First and foremost, sustainability requires us to raise the age of retirement. Most would probably advocate a return to age 65 as a benchmark target. There is much to be said for this: people begin their careers later, the health status of older workers is improving for each new cohort approaching retirement age, and the education gap that until now was huge between older and younger workers is rapidly closing. Put differently, there is good news both on the pull and push side. Workers are less compelled to retire for health reasons, and employers will be less eager to shed themselves of older personnel.

Our institutions need, however, to adapt to the postponement of retirement. Pension accruals in many countries' retirement systems implicitly urge workers to take early retirement. Also wage bargaining systems based on seniority wage hikes need to be changed to avoid older workers being priced out of the market. An extreme example is France where a 60-year-old worker, simply due to seniority, earns 40 per cent more than a worker aged 35. As pension entitlements are increasingly based on full-career earnings, rather than just the years immediately preceding retirement, the pressure behind seniority wages should ease considerably.

Delaying retirement is one logical ingredient in the Musgrave model for intergenerational equity. But it may threaten equity because life expectancy is positively related to social status. To pursue equity, we should accordingly link the age of retirement to a person's previous lifetime income. This would produce a double advantage for society as well since high-income persons are the most expensive pensioners but also the most productive workers. Hence, we save considerably on pension expenditure and gain additionally on tax revenues. The dilemma here is that high-income earners are likely to have large private pension savings that make them relatively immune to incentives in public schemes. The case for some harmonization of public and private pension plans is therefore evident.

As Guillemard (2003) so persuasively shows, the 'one-size-fits-all' model of retirement of the post-war era is no longer adequate. Its understanding of 'universality' was the product of the highly *standardized* life courses; of the uniformity of work lives in the age of high industrialism. The far more differentiated life courses of post-industrial economies, in particular as women's employment becomes the norm, require a different understanding of universality, one that allows for multiple and more flexible pathways into retirement, including active labour market and partial retirement instruments.

Maximizing employment is key to securing future pensions. Again, this is clearly also a principal ingredient in any sustainable 'Musgrave model'. The per capita additional burden that will fall on the 'young' will decline in proportion to the number of active workers. The attainment of maximum employment will mainly have to come from female labour supply. This is perhaps the least challenging ingredient in any future scenario, simply because female participation is growing very rapidly everywhere. Pissaridis et al. (2003) have argued that the Italian and Spanish pension systems may be more sustainable than one would think, simply because female employment in young cohorts is growing at an extraordinary pace.

Female employment may provoke new dilemmas about equity. It will help close the gap with men in terms of accumulated pension rights. But marital selection implies a widening income gap between high- and low-earner couples that will influence not only joint pension income but also the age of retirement.

Since the new economy is likely to create far greater heterogeneity and inequality of life chances, future retirees will, likewise, experience more inequality in terms of accumulated savings and entitlements. A good case can therefore be made in favour of some kind of basic, revenue-financed pension guarantee as the bottom tier of any pension regime. And if private pension plans will grow in importance, this will heighten the degree of insecurity attached to future retirement income. Here, then, is a second good case for a basic pension guarantee. From a financial perspective, a basic income guarantee, pegged just above the poverty line, would be surprisingly cheap. Myles (2002) shows that if this were to be implemented in any EU country today, the added cost to the exchequer would only amount to less than 0.1 per cent of GDP.

A basic pension guarantee has the added advantage of helping to diversify the financial base of pension expenditures. Payroll financing implies a relatively narrow (and potentially regressive) tax base and, indirectly, a narrow system of risk-sharing. And, as spending requirements will rise substantially over the next decades, so will payroll taxes and fixed labour costs.

A system overly reliant on payroll taxation has demonstrably adverse second-order effects in terms of distribution, equity and employment. Inducing more private pension plans will of course help to diversify the financial base, but these will hardly satisfy criteria of efficiency and equity and will also, most probably, generate more insecurity. If increased longevity is skewed in favour of the privileged and if, additionally, the current trend towards rising income inequality continues into the future, the case for more progressive financing (and taxation) of benefits is stronger than ever. And if our first priorities are equity and security in old age, it would be logical to propose that publicly financed programmes, in particular the guaranteed basic pension, should expand in direct proportion to the growth of private plans.

What I have described are general principles of how to achieve an equitable and sustainable burden-sharing in our increasingly aged societies. We must, however, never forget that the welfare of the aged is – and always will be – primarily the outcome of their life course. The human life course is changing dramatically, for good or worse, and it is above all becoming more heterogeneous. The requisites for a good working life are rising, in particular in terms of education, skills and abilities. And since these are sown very early in childhood, there is absolutely nothing frivolous about claiming that good retirement policy begins with babies.

An Afterword

From cradle to deathbed, citizens of today encounter the same kinds of life passages as did our fathers' and grandfathers' generations. As always, we play, learn, find a job, fall in love, have children, nurture them and then adjust to the empty nest, grow old and retire until, inevitably, we must meet our maker. One way to depict the human life course is that little of importance has changed. Another is to highlight the radical changes of life in the advanced world. The biographical markers may not have changed much, but we approach them differently; the human life course is far less standardized and predictable; we have invented a plethora of alternatives to the model of marriage and family that our grandparents adhered to. Childhood today is, paradoxically, both shorter and longer than in previous generations; children spend more of their years in institutions, increasingly from a very tender age, and they terminate their formative years much later. Nonetheless, they also appear to see more of their parents – certainly of their fathers. And latter-day fathers and mothers are clearly adopting different parenting practices in terms of both time dedication and content. The balance between Gary Becker's n and q has swung decisively in favour of the latter.

Radical change is nowhere more evident than in the ways we approach family life. Marriage no longer implies fertility automatically and, of course, vice versa. Nor is it a finality. Where, as in Scandinavia, unstable partnerships are the norm (many never marry), an average child can expect to have not only the usual four grandparents, but possibly eight or even twelve, all depending on the dynamics of repartnering among their biological fathers and mothers. This may provoke turmoil in the life of the child. On the up side, it creates a massive reservoir of social capital and an avalanche of presents at Christmas. Mother, of course, is no longer omnipresent in the children's early years. But her job seems not to be harmful for their welfare, nor does it seem to diminish the amount of attention bestowed upon them – on the contrary, mothers and fathers spend, together, more active time on their children than ever before. Housework and leisure are being sacrificed on the altar of children and careers. It is possible that today's parents are more inclined to live in a home that is dirty and messy. But of far greater importance, they adopt more gender-egalitarian ways of cleaning, nurturing and making ends meet.

As the feminists insist, we are still a long way off from true equality in either home production or working life. Whatever may lay ahead for gender equalization, be it in terms of degree or substance, all the evidence that I have examined in this book suggests that women are spearheading a new social order. We find ourselves caught in the midst of this process and have, accordingly, some difficulty fathoming where precisely it is heading. Contemporary societies seem to be based on multiple equilibria. We have not yet fully left the *ancien régime* behind, nor have we effectively forged its replacement. Accordingly, a large share of the population finds itself in an unstable equilibrium with the associated sub-optimal outcomes.

The fall of the *ancien régime* can be traced to multiple forces of change. My treatment has centred primarily on demographic transformation and on the aftershocks of the female revolution. I am persuaded that we confront a genuine revolution because it provokes a fundamental alteration of how citizens decide and behave along the entire lifespan, including education, marriage, family life, parenting and career dedication. I am additionally persuaded that the revolution, either directly or indirectly, embodies major structural change in terms of how our societies function. We have arguably exaggerated the influence of globalization and technology while paying too little attention to changes induced by the new demography. This is particularly the case for social inequalities.

The core thesis developed in this book is that the more incomplete the revolution, the greater are the inequalities in its wake. In some respects it may be warranted to speak of polarizing trends.

This occurs primarily because the revolution is spearheaded by women from the privileged social classes, the highly educated. It is only when it starts to seriously trickle down to the lower social strata that the revolution enters a state of maturity that, in turn, is a precondition for more egalitarian outcomes. Put bluntly, the quest for gender equality tends to produce social inequality as long as it is a middle-class affair.

From a disciplinary point of view the new inequalities present an odd paradox. Inequalities may be of little direct concern within mainstream economic theory and, yet, contemporary economics has produced a truly impressive amount of research on the subject. In contrast, social inequality has always been a core disciplinary concern in sociology. But, as several leading sociologists have recently observed, the brusque return of major inequalities seems to have passed the profession by. Serious sociological analyses of the changing distribution of income are hard to find.

There would, in fact, be little that a sociologist could contribute if the new inequalities were simply a derivative of technology-driven changes in the returns to human capital. This is undoubtedly the dominant – but certainly not the only – view within the economics literature. Many economists have, in fact, entered into the lacuna of sociological research. Some, like Burtless (1999) and Hyslop (2001), have examined how altered family patterns influence income distributions; others, like Goldin and Katz (2008), look at the effects of educational choices.

I think the economists have, in part, been studying the new inequalities for the wrong reasons, and also that the sociologists have ignored the issue due to a poor understanding of what is unfolding. Most of the research that comes from economics has been motivated by an interest in understanding the sudden changes in wage structures. Inevitably, economists have broached equity issues, whether tacitly or explicitly. This is perhaps clearest in the suddenly intensified interest in intergenerational mobility, but is no doubt also a major issue behind the voluminous work on early childhood investments, so much associated with James Heckman. Indeed, any economist who is seriously concerned with identifying superior win–win outcomes will, by definition, be compelled to confront equity head-on.

Ironically, the economics literature has only rarely – if at all – broached inequality from an efficiency point of view. This is quite odd since it is rather evident that mounting inequalities harbour potentially large inefficiencies. We are clearly misallocating our capital if the cost of eradicating child poverty is only one-tenth of the estimated GDP loss that can be ascribed to it. If more inequality produces less intergenerational mobility we suffer, once again, serious efficiency losses. Talent from the bottom is wasted and, as Heckman and others have shown, every dollar that we invest in early childhood has huge rates of return, especially for the least privileged children. It is, at the other end of the spectrum, similarly evident that we may be over-investing in rich but untalented kids so as to shelter them from downward mobility. The reader may recall Table 2.5 which shows that roughly 35 per cent of sons born into the top-income quintile manage to remain in the same quintile. This exceeds what one would statistically expect by 15 percentage points. It would be interesting to see an estimate of the economic resources that are funnelled into such anti-meritocratic expenditure.

And the sociologists err considerably if they maintain that the new inequalities lie outside their range of competences. A first clue comes from the recent contributions by economists, like Acemoglu (2002) or Goldin and Katz (2008), who suggest that the widening of wage differentials may have little to do with technologies but, instead, reflect cohort-specific trends in education. In the US, over the past decades, college enrolments have been stagnant despite intensifying demand for skills. Hence the rising returns to human capital. In Europe, in contrast, enrolments in higher education may have outpaced the rhythm of technology-based demand and this is why top earners here have not raced away from the rest of the pack. If this argumentation is persuasive, we face a truly enticing *sociological* puzzle, namely why are youth not responding to the increasingly clear signals that come from the market place? Why are youth in general, and boys in particular, not acting according to the rational choice manual and investing in more education so as to reap the benefits of skyrocketing human capital returns? This is an obvious question for sociologists to address.

In this book I have focused on a different complex of factors that are of relevance for any understanding of rising inequality.

I have tried to regain some of the disciplinary terrain lost to the economists by identifying how the demographic correlates of the female revolution are potentially very inequality-inducing. Changes in marital behaviour such as intensified homogamy among the highly educated, and the increasingly socially skewed incidence of divorce and single motherhood, have major repercussions across the income distribution. This garners, in turn, greater inequalities in parenting. Differentials in parents' spending on children are widening but, arguably worse, we detect growing gaps in nurturing behaviour, too. Roughly speaking, higher educated parents allot 30 per cent more time to their children than do the low educated. And these discrepancies are especially acute in 'developmental parenting', namely in those activities that most directly influence children's acquisition of skills.

There are two major reasons why ongoing trends point towards polarization. The first stems from recent research on intergenerational income mobility which demonstrates evident non-linearities across the income spectrum: too little upward mobility from the bottom and too little downward mobility from the top. Privilege and underprivilege are being systematically reproduced and the more that such a process intensifies, the greater will be the discrepancies in life chances. The second, and more important reason, is that this occurs according to a *cumulative* pattern. The distance between the top and bottom appears to be widening along an array of interconnected factors: family income, spending on children, and both the quantity and quality of parenting. As also emphasized in Sarah McLanahan's important article, aptly titled 'diverging destinies', such polarization will have major – and hugely problematic – consequences for the coming generations (McLanahan, 2004). In fact, we are sowing the seeds of a more stratified society in the future.

Here, then, we find once again an obviously relevant topic for sociological inquiry. What are the precise social mechanisms that promote cumulative inequalities? Why are there such large gaps in parenting? What are the processes of social selection that explain the uneven pace of gender equalization in home production? And, perhaps most importantly, why is a sometimes large segment of womanhood so reluctant to climb on the revolutionary wagon? By citing the perseverance of traditional gender norms, many sociologists believe they have provided an answer. This is, however, not an explanation but simply a description, right or wrong, of how men and women behave.

Post-war sociologists provided us with telling and persuasive insights concerning the social order that came together in the rich nations at mid-century. Writers like Seymour Lipset, Talcott Parsons and Daniel Bell portrayed what they believed was a new social equilibrium built on the cornerstones of the nuclear family, the end of polarizing ideologies and class strife, and the convergence around middle-class norms and life styles. They clearly erred seriously in believing that this equilibrium had staying power, that it marked the culmination of an essentially unidirectional evolutionary path. In the decades that followed we have seen the eclipse not only of the housewife, but also of the Parsonian family. The idyllic happy-middle-class society fails to resonate among contemporary social commentators who, instead, see fragmentation, social exclusion, the crystallization of an ultra-privileged class of super-achievers and, yes, social polarization. We have finally woken up to the fact that there has been no serious progress towards a genuine equality of opportunities.

Sociological analysis is, no doubt, stymied by the presence of an unstable equilibrium that offers unclear normative standards and strains our institutions. If this is the by-product of the female revolution, must we then await its completion in order to see more clearly the contours of whatever new social order lies beyond our horizons? Returning to a point made in the introduction to this book, I think that we social scientists can do much better than paste another 'post' onto tired old labels. But how might we go about it? One obvious way would be to direct our analytical lens to those societies where the revolution is most advanced. Which are they? One might, as many do, identify them in terms of women's incorporation in work-life. That would, however, be misleading. Female employment sets the stage for, but does not define, the revolution. As I insisted in chapter 1, a revolution implies decisive ruptures in the way that women *and* men go about their lives. It means that a new equilibrium is being forged. So as to avoid 'post'-labels, I term it the *gender-equality equilibrium*. We should therefore hone in on those societies where citizens from different social strata differ little in terms of adopting new marriage, fertility, divorce, employment and, not to forget, home production patterns. If social class differences become minor we would assume that the new normative framework is becoming hegemonic.

My empirical focus on North America and the Nordic countries follows this logic. These countries can serve as ideal typical images of what is crystallizing throughout the advanced world. In fact, my persistent focus also on laggard countries, in particular in Southern Europe, has been importantly motivated by the search for common principles of change – do the laggards follow the leaders? I think the evidence favours this view. Take the extraordinarily rapid pace of female incorporation in paid employment in Spain. This has been accompanied by an equally rapid change in spousal specialization. In fact, we must conclude that the portrait of Spanish family life as the epitome of traditionalism no longer holds. Young parents behave increasingly like Americans when it comes to who reads with the children or washes the dishes.

This book was inevitably driven towards a welfare state analysis, primarily because I came to see the importance of policy for the way that the female revolution unfolds. I am, in fact, persuaded that the attainment of a stable new gender-equality equilibrium requires a powerful exogenous trigger and that the welfare state remains the only credible trigger available. If so, how must our welfare states adapt? I think the answer is rather obvious, albeit not for the reasons routinely voiced by feminists. The real urgency comes from the inequality-producing consequences of the revolution as it winds its way towards maturity. And these consequences embrace the micro-world of family life as well as the macro-world of social integration; they touch upon every facet of our life course and, not to forget, of the life chances of future generations.

Yet a case for welfare state reform that bases itself solely on egalitarian motives will persuade only those who already agree. A far stronger case emerges when it can be demonstrated that policy reforms can move us to a superior Pareto frontier. This implies a win–win outcome in which more equity goes hand in hand with a more effective mobilization of our productive potential. A Paretian case for welfare state adaptation emerges with sufficient clarity, I believe, on many fronts. On all fronts it must be the case that alternative arrangements – essentially either the family or the market – will provide sub-optimal solutions.

With this set of minimalist criteria I believe, firstly, that I have made a fairly persuasive case for the welfare state in terms of reconciling motherhood and employment. In this case, the absence of welfare state support will result in one (or both) of two evils: too few children and/or too few workers and too little family income. I have also, I hope, made a case for greater intragenerational equity in retirement. In this second case the failure to ensure equity will jeopardize our increasingly urgent effort to postpone retirement. Failure to achieve the latter will, in turn, seriously jeopardize the sustainability of public finances and the intergenerational contract. But the single most persuasive case lies, no doubt, in child investments that will, at once, ensure greater equality of opportunities and major productivity gains. And investing well in early childhood provides also excellent insurance against poverty and need in old age. And, to conclude, if the welfare state can help accelerate the revolution of women's roles, we will probably also harvest major equality and efficiency gains across the board.

References

Aaberge, R., Columbino, U. and del Boca, D. (2005), 'Women's participation in the labour market and fertility', in T. Boeri, D. del Boca and C. Pissaridis (eds), *Women at Work: An Economic Perspective*. Oxford: Oxford University Press, pp. 121–239.

Aaronson, S. (2002), 'The rise in lifetime earnings inequality among men'. Unpublished manuscript, *Board of Governors of the Federal Reserve System*, Washington, DC.

Acemoglu, D. (2002), 'Cross-country inequality trends'. *LIS Working Paper*, no. 296 (March).

Adema, W. and Ledaique, V. (2005), 'Net social expenditure, 2005 edition'. *OECD Social, Employment and Migration Working Paper*, 29.

Aguiar, M. and Hurst, E. (2006), 'Measuring trends in leisure: The allocation of time over five decades'. *NBER Working Paper*, 12082 (March).

Ahn, N. and Mira, P. (2002), 'A note on the changing relationship between fertility and female employment rates in developed countries'. *Journal of Population Economics*, 15: 667–82.

Alvarez, B. and Miles, D. (2003), 'Gender effect on housework allocation: Evidence from Spanish two-earner couples'. *Journal of Population Economics*, 16: 227–42.

Andersson, B. (1992), 'Effects of day care on cognitive and socioemotional competence of 13-year-old Swedish schoolchildren'. *Child Development*, 63: 20–36.

Anderson, P. and Levine, P. (2000), 'Childcare and mothers' employment decisions', in D. Card and R. Blank (eds), *Finding Jobs*. New York: Russell Sage.

Atkinson, A. (1995), 'Is the welfare state necessarily an obstacle to economic growth?' *European Economic Review*, 39: 723–30.

Atkinson, A. B. (1999), 'Is rising income inequality inevitable? A critique of the transatlantic consensus'. Annual Lecture, United Nations University.

Atkinson, A. and Viby-Mogensen, G. (1993), *Welfare and Work Incentives*. Oxford: Clarendon Press.

Bane, M. J. (1974), *Here to Stay: American Families in the Twentieth Century*. New York: Basic Books.

Barnett, W. and Belfield, C. (2006), 'Early childhood development and social mobility'. *The Future of Children*, 16: 73–98.

Barr, N. (1998), *The Economics of the Welfare State*. Stanford, CA: Stanford University Press.

Barr, N. (2001), *The Welfare State as a Piggy Bank: Information, Risk, Uncertainty and the Role of the State*. Oxford: Oxford University Press.

Beaujot, R. (2000), *Earning and Caring in Canadian Families*. Peterborough: Broadview.

Beaujot, R. (2004), 'Delayed life transitions: Trends and implications', Ottawa: The Vanier Institute of the Family, pp. 1–46.

Beblo, M. and Wolf, E. (2002), 'How much does a year off cost? Estimating the wage effects of employment breaks and part-time periods'. *Cahiers Economiques de Bruxelles*, 45: 191–217.

Becker, G. (1981), *A Treatise on the Family*. Cambridge, MA: Harvard University Press.

Becker, G. and Lewis, H. (1973), 'On the interaction between quantity and quality of children'. *Journal of Political Economy*, 81: 279–88.

Becker, G. and Tomes, N. (1986), 'Human capital and the rise and fall of families'. *Journal of Labor Economics*, 4: 1–39.

Berk, S. (1985), *The Gender Factory*. New York: Plenum Press.

Bernal, R. and Keane, M. (2005), 'Maternal time, child care and child cognitive development. The case of single mothers'. Unpublished paper, Department of Economics, Northwestern University (September 15).

Bernardi, F. (1999), 'Does the husband matter? Married women's employment in Italy'. *European Sociological Review*, 15: 285–300.

Bernardi, F. (2005), 'Public policies and low fertility'. *Journal of European Social Policy*, 15: 123–38.

Bianchi, S. (2000), 'Maternal employment and time with children'. *Demography*, 37: 401–14.

Bianchi, S., Casper, L. and Peltola, P. (1996), 'A cross-national look at married women's economic dependency'. *LIS Working Paper Series*, no. 143.

Bianchi, S., Milkie, M., Sayer, L. and Robinson, J. (2000), 'Is anyone doing the housework? Trends in the gender division of household labor'. *Social Forces*, 79: 191–228.

Bianchi, S., Cohen, P., Raley, S. and Nomaguchi, K. (2004), 'Inequality in parental investment in child-rearing', in K. Neckerman (ed.), *Social*

Inequality. New York: Russell Sage, pp. 189–219.

Bianchi, S., Robinson, J. and Milkie, M. (2006), *Changing Rhythms of American Family Life*. New York: Russell Sage.

Biblarz, T. and Raftery, A. (1999), 'Family structure, educational attainment and socioeconomic success'. *American Journal of Sociology*, 105(2): 321–65.

Billari, F., Castiglioni, M., Castro Martin, T., Michielin, F. and Ongaro, B. (2002), 'Household and union formation in a Mediterranean fashion', in M. Corijn and E. Klijzing (eds), *Dynamics of Fertility and Partnership in Europe: Insights and Lessons from Comparative Research*, Vol. 2. Geneva: United Nations.

Bittman, M., England, P., Sayer, L., Folbre, N. and Matheson, G. (2003), 'When does gender trump money? Bargaining and time in household work'. *American Journal of Sociology*, 109: 186–214.

Bjorklund, A. and Palme, M. (2002), 'Income distribution within the life cycle versus between individuals', in D. Cohen, T. Piketty and G. Saint Paul (eds), *The Economics of Rising Inequalities*. Oxford: Oxford University Press, pp. 171–204.

Bjorklund, A., Jantti, M. and Solon, G. (2005), 'Influences of nature and nurture on earnings variation', in S. Bowles, H. Gintis and M. Osborne (eds), *Unequal Chances*. New York: Russell Sage, pp. 145–64.

Blackburn, M. L. and Bloom, D. (1989), 'Income inequality, business cycles and female labour supply', *Research in Economic Inequality*, Vol. 1, Greenwich, CT: JAI Press.

Blanden, J., Goodman, A., Gregg, P. and Machin, S. (2004), 'Changes in intergenerational mobility in Britain', in M. Corak (ed.), *Generational Income Mobility in North America and Europe*. Cambridge: Cambridge University Press, pp. 122–46.

Blau, D. (2001), *The Child Care Problem: An Economic Analysis*. New York: Russell Sage.

Blau, D. and Robins, P. (1989), 'Fertility, employment and childcare costs'. *Demography*, 26(2): 374–81.

Blau, F. and Kahn, L. (2003), 'Understanding international differences in the gender pay gap'. *Journal of Labor Economics*, 21(1): 106–44.

Blau, F. and Kahn, L. (2007), 'Changes in the labor supply behavior of married women, 1980–2000'. *Journal of Labor Economics*, 25: 393–48.

Blau, F., Brinton, M. and Grusky, D. (2006), *The Declining Significance of Gender?* New York: Russell Sage.

Blau, F., Ferber, M. and Winkler, A. (1998), *The Economics of Men, Women and Work*. New Jersey: Prentice Hall.

Bloemen, H. and Stancanelli, E. (2008), 'Housework, child care and paid work of spouses: Are wage rates the driving factor?' Unpublished paper, Department of Economics, Free University of Amsterdam (April).

Blossfeld, H. P. and Drobnic, S. (2001), *Careers of Couples in Contemporary Society*. Oxford: Oxford University Press.

Blossfeld, H. P. and Hakim, C. (1997), *Between Equalization and Marginalization*. Oxford: Oxford University Press.

Blossfeld, H. P. and Timm, A. (2003), *Who Marries Whom?* Dortrecht: Kluwer Publications.

Boeri, T., del Boca, D. and Pissaridis, C. (2005), *Women at Work: An Economic Perspective*. Oxford: Oxford University Press.

Bonke, J. and Esping-Andersen, G. (2008), 'Productivities, preferences and parental child care'. *Demosoc Working Paper*, 29, Universitat Pompeu Fabra.

Bonke, J., Datta Gupta, N. and Smith, N. (2003), 'The effect of timing and flexibility of housework activities on the wages of Danish men and women'. Unpublished paper, Danish Institute for Social Research (March 20).

Bose, C. (ed.) (1987), *The Hidden Aspects of Women's Work*. New York: Praeger.

Bourdieu, P. (1977), *Reproduction in Education, Society and Culture*. Beverly Hills: Sage.

Bourdieu, P. (1983), 'The forms of capital', in J. Richardson (ed.), *Handbook of Theory and Research in the Sociology of Education*. Westport, CT: Greenwood.

Bowles, S., Gintis, H. and Osborne, M. (2001), 'The determinants of earnings: A behavioural approach'. *Journal of Economic Literature*, XXXIX: 1137–76.

Bowles, S., Gintis, H. and Osborne Groves, M. (2005), *Unequal Chances: Family Background and Economic Success*. New York: Russell Sage.

Bowlus, A. and Robin, J. M. (2003), 'Twenty years of rising inequality in US lifetime labor income values'. Unpublished paper (www.restud.org.uk/barlusrobin-res.pdf)

Bratberg, E., Nilsen, O. and Vaage, K. (2005), 'Intergenerational earnings mobility in Norway'. *Scandinavian Journal of Economics*, 107(3): 419–35.

Breen, R. (2001). 'A rational choice model of educational inequality'. *Instituto Juan March Working Paper*. Vol. 166 (October), pp. 1–29.

Breen, R. (ed.) (2004), *Social Mobility in Europe*. Oxford: Oxford University Press.

Breen, R. and Cooke, L. (2005), 'The persistence of the gendered division of domestic labour'. *European Sociological Review*, 21: 43–57.

Brines, J. (1994), 'Economic dependency, gender, and the division of labor at home'. *American Journal of Sociology*, 100: 652–88.

Brodmann, S., Esping-Andersen, G. and Guell, M. (2007), 'When fertility is bargained'. *European Sociological Review*, 23: 599–614.

Brooks-Gunn, J., Duncan, G. and Aber, L. (1997), *Neighborhood Poverty: Context and Consequences for Children*, Vol. 1. New York: Russell Sage.

Browning, M. (1992), 'Children and household economic behavior'. *Journal of Economic Literature*, XXX (September 1992): 1434–75.

Browning, M., Bourguignon, F., Chiappori, P.-A. and Lechene, V. (1994), 'Incomes and outcomes: A structural model of within household allocation'. *Journal of Political Economy*, 102(6): 1067–96.

Burtless, G. (1999), 'Effects of growing wage disparities and changing family composition on the US income distribution'. *European Economic Review*, 43: 853–65.

Burtless, G. and Quinn, J. (2001), 'Retirement trends and policies to encourage work among older Americans', in Peter Budetti, Richard Burkhauser, Janice Gregory and H. Allan Hunt (eds), *Ensuring Health and Income Security for an Aging Workforce*, Kalamazoo, MI: Upjohn Institute, pp. 375–416.

Butrica, B., Iams, H. and Smith, K. (2003), 'It's all relative: understanding the retirement prospects of the baby-boomers'. Center for Retirement Research at Boston College, *Working Paper 2003–21*, Boston.

Calhoun, C. and Espenshade, T. (1988), 'Childbearing and wives' foregone earnings'. *Population Studies*, 43(1): 5–38.

Cambois, E., Robine, J. M. and Hayward, M. (2001), 'Social inequalities in disability-free life expectancy in the French male population, 1980–1991'. *Demography*, 38: 513–24.

Cancian, M., and Reed, D. (1999), 'The impact of wives' earnings on income inequality: issues and estimates'. *Demography*, 36(2): 173–84.

Cancian, M., Danziger, S. and Gottschalk, P. (1993), 'The changing contributions of men and women to the level of and distribution of family income: 1968–1988', in D. Papadimitrou and E. Wolff (eds), *Poverty and Prosperity in the USA in the Late 20th Century*. London: Macmillan Press, pp. 320–55.

Card, D. (1999), 'The causal effect of education on earnings', in Orley Ashenfelter and David Card (eds), *Handbook of Labor Economics*, Vol. 3A. Amsterdam: Elsevier Science, pp. 1801–64.

Carneiro, P. and Heckman, J. (2003), 'Human capital policy', in J. Heckman and A. Krueger (eds), *Inequality in America*. Cambridge, MA: MIT Press.

Castells, M. (1996), *The Rise of the Network Society*. Oxford: Blackwell.

CERC (2004), *Child Poverty in France*. Paris: Conseil de L'Emploi, des Revenues et de la Cohesion Sociale (Report number 4).

Cherlin, A. (1992), *Marriage, Divorce, and Remarriage*. Cambridge, MA: Harvard University Press.

Chiappori, P. (1988), 'Rational household labor supply'. *Econometrica*, 56: 63–90.

Chiappori, P. (1992), 'Collective labor supply and welfare'. *Journal of Political Economy*, 100: 437–67.

Christoffersen, N. (1993), *Familien I Aendring. En Statistisk Belysning af Familieforholdene*. Copenhagen: SFI.

Coleman, J. (1988), 'Social capital in the creation of human capital'. *American Journal of Sociology*, 94: 95–121.

Cooke, L. P. (2004), 'The gendered division of labour and family outcomes in Germany'. *Journal of Marriage and the Family*, 66: 1246–59.

Cooke, L. P. (2006), '"Doing" gender in context: Household bargaining and risk of divorce in Germany and the United States'. *American Journal of Sociology*, 112(2) (September 2006): 442–72.

Cooke, L. P. (forthcoming), 'Gender equity and fertility in Italy and Spain'. *Journal of Social Policy*.

Corak, M. (2004), *Generational Income Mobility in North America and Europe*. Cambridge: Cambridge University Press.

Corak, M. (2005), 'Do poor children become poor adults?' Paper prepared for the *CRISS Workshop*, Siena (September 25–6).

Cordon, F. and Sgritta, G. (2000), 'A Mediterranean perspective on low fertility'. Paper presented at the *European Observatory on Family*. Sevilla (September 15–16).

Corijn, M. and Klijzing, E. (eds) (2001), *Transition to Adulthood in Europe*. Dordrecht: Kluwer.

Couch, K. and Lillard, D. (2004), 'Non-linear patterns of intergenerational mobility on Germany and the United States', in M. Corak (ed.), *Generational Income Mobility*. Cambridge: Cambridge University Press, pp. 190–206.

Council of Europe (2001), *Recent Demographic Transformations in Europe*. Strasbourg: Council of Europe.

Currie, J. (2001), 'Early childhood intervention programs'. *Journal of Economic Perspectives*, 15: 213–38.

Datta Gupta, N. and Smith, N. (2002), 'Children and career interruptions: The family gap in Denmark'. *Economica*, 69: 609–29.

Davies, J. and Shorrocks, A. (1999), 'The distribution of wealth', in A. Atkinson and F. Bourguignon (eds), *Handbook of Income Distribution*, Vol. 1. Amsterdam: Elsevier, pp. 605–75.

Davies, J., Zhang, J. and Zeng, J. (2005), 'Intergenerational mobility under private vs. public education'. *Scandinavian Journal of Economics*, 107(3): 399–417.

Deding, M. and Lausten, M. (2004), 'Choosing between his time and her time?' Unpublished paper, *Danish Institute for Social Research* (March).

De Graaf, P. (1998), 'Parents' financial and cultural resources, grades, and transitions to secondary school'. *European Sociological Review*, 4: 209–21.

DeLaat, J. and Sevilla Sanz, A. (2006), 'Working women, men's home time and lowest-low fertility'. *ISER Working Paper*, 23.

Del Boca, D. (2003), 'The effect of child care and part-time opportunities on participation and fertility'. *Journal of Population Economics*, 15: 549–73.

Del Boca, D. and Pasqua, S. (2002), 'Employment patterns of husbands and wives and family income distribution in Italy (1977–1998)', IZA Discussion Papers 489, Institute for the Study of Labor (IZA).

De Santis, G. (2004), 'The monetary cost of children'. *Genus*, LX(1): 161–83.

Dex, S., Ward, D. and Joshi, H. (2008), 'Changes in women's occupations and occupational mobility over 25 years', in J. Scott, S. Dex and H. Joshi (eds), *Women and Employment: Changing Lives and New Challenges*. Cheltenham: Edward Elgar, pp. 54–80.

Duncan, G. and Brooks-Gunn, J. (1997), *Consequences of Growing Up Poor*. New York: Russell Sage.

Duvander, A. and Andersson, G. (2003), 'Gender equality and fertility in Sweden', in R. Erikson and J. Jonsson (1996), *Can Education be Equalized? The Swedish Case in Comparative Perspective*. Boulder, CO: Westview Press.

Ellwood, D. and Jencks, C. (2004), 'The spread of single-parent families in the United States since 1960', in D. Moynihan, T. Smeeding and L. Rainwater (eds), *The Future of the Family*. New York: Russell Sage, pp. 25–65.

England, P. and Budig, M. (1998), 'Gary Becker on the family', in D. Clawson (ed.), *Required Reading: Sociology's Most Influential Books*. Amherst: University of Massachusetts Press, pp. 99–110.

England, P. and Farkas, G. (1986), *Households, Employment and Gender.* New York: Aldine.

Erikson, R. and Goldthorpe, J. (1992), *The Constant Flux.* Oxford: Clarendon Press.

Erikson, R. and Jonsson, J. (1996), *Can Education be Equalized? The Swedish Case in Comparative Perspective.* Boulder, CO: Westview Press.

Ermisch, J. (1988), 'The econometric analysis of birth rate dynamics in Britain'. *Journal of Human Resources*, 23(4): 563–76.

Ermisch, J. (2003), 'How do parents affect the life chances of their children as adults? An idiosyncratic view'. SEDAP Research Paper No. 101, McMaster University, Hamilton, ON.

Ermisch, J. and Francesconi, M. (2002), 'The effect of parents' employment on children's educational attainment'. *ISER Working Paper*, 21, University of Essex.

Esping-Andersen, G. (1999), *Social Foundations of Postindustrial Economies.* Oxford: Oxford University Press.

Esping-Andersen, G. (2002), 'A child-centred social investment strategy', in G. Esping-Andersen, D. Gallie, A. Hemerijck and J. Myles (eds), *Why We Need a New Welfare State.* Oxford: Oxford University Press, pp. 26–67.

Esping-Andersen, G. (2004), 'Untying the Gordian knot of social inheritance'. *Research in Social Stratification and Mobility*, 21: 115–38.

Esping-Andersen, G. (2005), 'Inequality of incomes and opportunities', in A. Giddens and P. Diamond (eds), *The New Egalitarianism: Opportunity and Prosperity in Modern Societies.* Cambridge: Polity, pp. 8–38.

Esping-Andersen, G. (2007), 'Sociological explanations of changing income distributions'. *American Behavioral Scientist*, 50: 639–58.

Esping-Andersen, G., Gallie, D., Hemerijck, A. and Myles, J. (2002), *Why We Need a New Welfare State.* Oxford: Oxford University Press.

Esping-Andersen, G. and Myles, J. (2008), 'The welfare state and redistribution.' Ch. 14 in *The Oxford Handbook of Economic Inequality.* Oxford: Oxford University Press.

Evers, A., Lewis, J. and Riedel, B. (2005), 'Developing childcare provision in England and Germany'. *Journal of European Social Policy*, 15: 195–210.

Evertsson, M. and Nermo, M. (2004), 'Dependence within families and the division of labor'. *Journal of Marriage and the Family*, 66: 1272–86.

Evertsson, M. and Nermo, M. (2007), 'Changing resources and the division of housework'. *European Sociological Review*, 23: 455–70.

Farkas, G. (2003), 'Cognitive skills and noncognitive traits and behaviours in stratification process'. *Annual Review of Sociology*, 29: 541–62.

Felfe, A. C. (2008), *Economic Consequences of Motherhood – The Role of Disamenities*. PhD thesis, Department of Economics, Universitat Pompeu Fabra (July).

Fernandez, R., Guner, N. and Knowles, J. (2005), 'Love or money: A theoretical and empirical analysis of household sorting and inequality'. *Quarterly Journal of Economics*, 120(1): 273–344.

Ferree, M. (1990), 'Beyond separate spheres: Feminism and family research'. *Journal of Marriage and the Family*, 54: 866–84.

Feyrer, J., Sacerdote, B. and Stern, A. (2008), 'Will the stork return to Europe and Japan?' *Journal of Economic Perspectives*, 22 (3): 3-2A(0).

Forster, M. and d'Ercole, M. (2005), 'Income distribution and poverty in OECD countries in the second half of the 1990s'. *OECD Social, Employment and Migration Working Paper*, no. 22.

Fritzell, J. and Henz, U. (2001), 'Household income dynamics', in J. Jonsson and C. Mills (eds), *Cradle to Grave: Life Course Change in Sweden*, Durham: Sociology Press, pp. 184–210.

Fuchs, V. (1988), *Women's Quest for Economic Equality*. Cambridge, MA: Harvard University Press.

Fuwa, M. (2004), 'Macro-level gender inequality and the division of household labor in 22 countries'. *American Sociological Review*, 69: 751–67.

Garrett, G. (1998), 'Global markets and national politics: collision course or virtuous circle?' *International Organization*, 52: 787–824.

Gauthier, A. and Hatzius, J. (1997), 'Family benefits and fertility: an econometric analysis'. *Population Studies*, 38(3): 295–306.

Gauthier, A. and Lelievre, E. (1994), 'Women's employment patterns in Europe'. Paper presented at the *Comparing Welfare Systems in Europe Conference*, Oxford University, May 20–22.

Geist, C. (2005), 'The welfare state and the home'. *European Sociological Review*, 21: 23–41.

Gershuny, J. (2000), *Changing Times. Work and Leisure in Postindustrial Society*. Oxford: Oxford University Press.

Gershuny, J. and Robinson, J. (1988), 'Historical changes in the household division of labour'. *Demography*, 25: 537–52.

Gershuny, J., Bittman, M. and Brice, J. (2005), 'Exit, voice, and suffering: do couples adapt to changing employment patterns?' *Journal of Marriage and the Family*, 67: 656–65.

184

Gershuny, J., Goodwin, M. and Jones, S. (1994), 'The domestic labour revolution' in M. Anderson, F. Bechhofer and J. Gershuny (eds), *The Social and Political Economy of the Household*. Oxford: Oxford University Press.

Ghysels, J. (2004), *Work, Family and Child Care*. Cheltenham: Edward Elgar.

Gittleman, M. and Joyce, M. (1999), 'Have family income mobility patterns changed?' *Demography*, 36: 299–314.

Giuseppe, B., Blau, F. and Kahn, L. (2002), 'Labor market institutions and demographic employment patterns'. *NBER Working Papers* 9043, National Bureau of Economic Research.

Goldin, C. (1990), *Understanding the Gender Gap*. Oxford: Oxford University Press.

Goldin, C. (2006), 'The quiet revolution that transformed women's employment, education, and family'. *American Economic Review*, 96: 1–21.

Goldin, C. and Katz, L. (2008), *The Race Between Education and Technology*. Cambridge, MA: Belknap Press.

Goldin, C., Katz, L. and Kuziemko, I. (2006), 'The homecoming of American college women: the reversal of the college gender gap'. *Journal of Economic Perspectives*, 20: 133–56.

Gonzalez, M. and Jurado, T. (2005), 'Is there a minimal set of conditions before having a baby?' *DEMOSOC Working Paper*, Universitat Pompeu Fabra (June).

Gornick, J. and Meyers, M. (2003), *Families that Work*. New York: Russell Sage Foundation.

Gottschalk, P. and Smeeding, T. (1997), 'Cross-national comparisons of earnings and income inequality'. *Journal of Economic Literature*, XXXV: 633–87.

Green, D. and Riddell, W. (2001), 'Literacy, numeracy and labour market outcomes in Canada'. Ottowa: Statistics Canada, catalogue no. 89-552-MIE, no. 8.

Green, D. and Riddell, W. (2003), 'Literacy and earnings'. *Labour Economics*, 10: 165–84.

Gregg, P. and Machin, S. (2001), 'Childhood experiences, educational attainment and adult labour market performance', in K. Vleminckx and T. Smeeding (eds), *Child Well-Being, Child Poverty and Child Policy in Modern Nations*. Bristol: Policy Press, pp. 129–50.

Gregg, P. and Wadsworth, J. (2001), 'Everything you ever wanted to know about worklessness and polarization at the household level but were afraid to ask'. *Oxford Bulletin of Economics and Statistics*, 63: 777–806.

Gregg, P., Harkness, S. and Machin, S. (1999), *Child Development and Family Income*. York: Joseph Rowntree Foundation.

Gregg, P., Washbrook, E., Propper, C. and Burgess, S. (2005), 'The effects of mothers' return to work decision on child development in the UK'. *The Economic Journal*, 115: 48–80.

Gregory, M. (2008), 'Gender and economic inequality', Ch. 12, in *The Oxford Handbook of Economic Inequality*. Oxford: Oxford University Press.

Grunow, D., Schulz, F. and Blossfeld, H. P. (2008), 'Gender norms and economic resources: what determines the division of housework in the course of marriage?' Unpublished paper, Department of Sociology, Yale University.

Guillemard, Anne-Marie (2003), *L'âge de l'emploi: Les sociétés à l'épreuve du vieillissement*. Paris: Armand Colin.

Gupta, S. (1999), 'The effects of transitions in marital status on men's performance of housework'. *Journal of Marriage and Family*, 61: 700–11.

Gustafsson, S. (2001), 'Optimal age at motherhood: theoretical and empirical considerations on postponement of maternity in Europe'. *Journal of Population Economics*, 14(2): 225–47.

Gustafsson, S. and Kenjoh, E. (2004), 'New evidence on work among new mothers'. *European Review of Labour and Research*, 10: 34–47.

Gustafsson, S. and Stafford, F. (1992), 'Child care subsidies and labour supply in Sweden'. *Journal of Human Resources*, 27: 204–30.

Gutierrez-Domenech, M. (2007), 'El tiempo con los hijos y la actividad laboral de los padres'. *La Caixa, Servicio de Estudios*, 6 (April).

Haber, C. and Gratton, B. (1994), *Old Age and the Search for Security: An American Social History*. Bloomington: Indiana University Press.

Haider, S. (2001), 'Earnings instability and earnings inequality of males in the United States, 1967–1991'. *Journal of Labor Economics*, 19: 799–836.

Hakim, C. (1996), *Key Issues in Women's Work*. London: Athlone.

Hakim, C. (2003), *Work-Lifestyle Choices in the Twenty-First Century*. Oxford: Oxford University Press.

Hallberg, D. and Klevmarken, A. (2003), 'Time for children: A study of parents' time allocation'. *Population Economics*, 16: 205–26.

Hanusheck, E., Kain, J., Markman, J. and Rivkin, S. (2003), 'Does peer ability affect student achievement?' *Journal of Applied Econometrics*, 18: 527–44.

Harding, D., Jencks, C., Lopoo, L. and Mayer, S. (2005), 'The changing effect of family background on the incomes of American adults', in

S. Bowles, H. Gintis and M. Osborne (eds), *Unequal Chances*. New York: Russell Sage, pp. 100–44.

Harkness, S. and Waldfogel, J. (2003), 'The family gap in pay: Evidence from seven industrialized countries'. *Research in Labor Economics*, 22: 369–414.

Hattersley, Lin (1999), 'Trends in life expectancy by social class – an update'. *Health Statistics Quarterly* 2: 16–24.

Haveman, R. and Wolfe, B. (1995), *Succeeding Generations: On the Effects of Investments in Children*. New York: Russell Sage Foundation.

Haveman, R., Sandefur, G., Wolfe, B. and Voyer, A. (2004), 'Trends in children's attainments', in K. Neckerman (ed.), *Social Inequality*. New York: Russell Sage, pp. 149–88.

Heckman, J. (1999), 'Doing it right: job training and education'. *The Public Interest* (Spring): 86–106.

Heckman, J. and Lochner, L. (2000), 'Rethinking education and training policy: understanding the sources of skill formation in a modern economy', in S. Danziger and J. Waldvogel (eds), *Securing the Future*. New York: Russell Sage, pp. 47–86.

Heclo, H. (1988), 'Generational politics', in John Palmer, Timothy Smeeding and Barbara Torrey (eds), *The Vulnerable*. Washington DC: The Urban Institute, pp. 381–411.

Hemerijck, A. (2002), 'The self-transformation of the European social models', in G. Esping-Andersen, A. Hemerijck and J. Myles (eds), *Why We Need a New Welfare State*. Oxford: Oxford University Press, pp. 173–214.

Hill, C. R. and Stafford, F. P. (1974), 'Allocation of time to pre-school children and educational opportunity'. *Journal of Human Resources*, 9(3): 323–41.

Hill, C. R. and Stafford, F. P. (1980), 'Parental care of children: Time diary estimates of quantity, predictability, and variety'. *Journal of Human Resources*, 15(2): 219–39.

Hills, J. (2004), *Inequality and the State*. Oxford: Oxford University Press.

Hochchild, A. (1989), *The Second Shift*. New York: Avon Books.

Hoem, B. (1995), 'The gender-segregated Swedish labor market', in V. Oppenheimer and A. Jensen (eds), *Gender and Family Change in Industrialized Countries*. Oxford: Clarendon Press, pp. 279–96.

Hook, J. (2006), 'Men's unpaid work in 20 countries, 1965–1998'. *American Sociological Review*, 71: 639–60.

Hotz, V. J., Klerman, J. A. and Willis, R. (1997), 'The economics of fertility in developed countries', in M. Rosenzweig and O. Stark (eds),

Handbook of Population and Family Economics, Vol. 1A. Amsterdam: Elsevier, pp. 276–347.

Huisman, M., Kunst, A. and Bopp, M. (2005), 'Educational inequalities in cause-specific mortality'. *Lancet*, 366: 807–8.

Hyslop, D. (2001), 'Rising U.S. earnings inequality and family labor supply: the covariance structure of intrafamily earnings'. *American Economic Review*, 91(4): 755–7.

Immervoll, H. and Barber, D. (2005), 'Can parents afford to work?' OECD-DELSA *Working Paper*, no. 10.

Iyigun, M. (2005), 'Bargaining and specialization in marriage'. *IZA Working Paper*, no. 1744.

Jacobzone, S. (1999), 'Ageing and caring for frail elderly persons: A review of international perspectives'. *Labour Market and Social Policy Occasional Paper*, OECD.

James-Burduny, S. (2005), 'The effect of maternal labor force participation on child development'. *Journal of Labor Economics*, 23(1): 177–211.

Jantti, M., Bratsberg, M., Roed, K., Raaum, R., Naylor, R., Osterbacka, E., Bjorklund, A. and Eriksson, T. (2006), 'American exceptionalism in a new light: A comparison of intergenerational earnings mobility in the Nordic countries, the United Kingdom, and the United States'. IZA Discussion Paper, no.1938, IZA-Bonn.

Jenkins, S. (1995), 'Accounting for inequality trends: Decomposition analysis for the UK, 1971–86'. *Economica*, 62: 29–63.

Jensen, P. (2002), 'The postponement of childbirth: Does it lead to a decline in completed fertility or is there a catch-up effect?' Unpublished paper, Department of Economics, Aarhus University (November).

Joshi, H., Davies, H. and Land, H. (1996), *The Tale of Mrs Typical*. London: Family Policy Studies Centre.

Juhn, C. and Murphy, K. (1997), 'Wage inequality and family labor supply'. *Journal of Labor Economics*, 15(1): 72–97.

Juhn, C., Murphy, K. and Pierce, B. (1993), 'Inequality and rise in returns to skills'. *Journal of Political Economy*, 101: 410–42.

Juster, T. and Stafford, F. (1985), *Time, Goods and Well-Being*. Ann Arbor, MI: University of Michigan Press.

Kamerman, S., Neuman, M., Waldfogel, J. and Brooks-Gunn, J. (2003), 'Social policy, family types, and child outcomes in selected OECD countries'. OECD Employment and Social Affairs *Working Paper*, no. 6.

Kampmann, J. and Warming Nielsen, H. (2004), 'Socialized childhood: Children in Denmark', in A. Jensen, A. Ben-Arieh, C. Conti,

D. Kutsar and H. Warming Nielsen (eds), *Children's Welfare in Ageing Europe*. Oslo: Norwegian Centre for Child Research, pp. 649–701.

Kangas, O. and Ritakallo, V. (1998), 'Social policy or structure? Income transfers, socioeconomic factors and poverty in the Nordic countries and France'. *LIS Working Paper*, 190.

Karoly, L. (1998), *Investing in our Children: What We Know and Don't Know About the Benefits of Early Childhood Investment*. Santa Monica, CA: Rand Corporation.

Karoly, L. and Burtless, G. (1995), 'Demographic change, rising earnings inequality, and the distribution of personal well-being, 1959–1989'. *Demography*, 32(3): 379–405.

Karoly, L., Kilburn, R, and Cannon, J. (2005), *Early Childhood Interventions*. Santa Monica, CA: Rand Corporation.

Katz, L. and Autor, D. (1999), 'Changes in the wage structure and earnings inequality', in O. Ashenfelter and D. Card (eds), *Handbook of Labor Economics*, Vol. 3A. Amsterdam: Elsevier, pp. 1464–1555.

Katzenstein, P. (1984), *Small States in World Markets*. Ithaca, NY: Cornell University Press.

Kenworthy, L. and Pontusson, J. (2005), 'Rising inequality and the politics of redistribution in affluent countries'. *Perspectives on Politics* 3(3): 449–71.

Kiernan, K. (2004), 'Unmarried co-habitation and parenthood', in D. Moynihan, T. Smeeding and L. Rainwater (eds), *The Future of the Family*. New York: Russell Sage, pp. 66–95.

Kim, K. and Rodriguez-Pueblita, J. (2005), 'Are married women secondary workers?' *Congressional Budget Office Working Paper*, 2005–11. Washington DC.

Klerman, J. and Karoly, L. (1994), 'Young men and the transition to stable employment'. *Monthly Labour Review*, 117: 31–48.

Klevmarken, A. (1998), 'Microeconomic analyses of time-use data. Did we reach the promised land?' Unpublished paper. Department of Economics, Uppsala University (May 15).

Knesebeck, O., Wahrendorf, M., Hyde, M. and Siegrist, J. (2007), 'Socioeconomic position and quality of life among older people in 10 European countries'. *Ageing and Society*, 27: 269–84.

Knudsen, L. (1999), 'Recent fertility trends in Denmark: The impact of family policy in a period of increasing fertility'. *Danish Centre for Demographic Research*, Research Report, no 11.

Kohler, H. P., Billari, F., and Ortega, J. A. (2002), 'The emergence of lowest-low fertility in Europe'. *Population and Development Review*, 28(4): 641–80.

Kohli, M., Guillemard, A., van Gunstern, H. and Rein, M. (1991), *Time for Retirement*. Cambridge: Cambridge University Press.

Korpi, T. and Stern, C. (2008), 'Globalization, deindustrialization and the labor market experiences of Swedish women', in H. P. Blossfeld and H. Hofmeister (eds), *Globalization, Uncertainty and Women's Careers*. Cheltenham: Edward Elgar, pp. 115–41.

Kravdal, O. (1996), 'How the local supply of daycare influences fertility in Norway'. *Population Research and Policy Review*, 15(3): 201–18.

Kravdal, O. and Rindfuss, R. (2008), 'Changing relationships between education and fertility: A study of women and men born 1940 to 1964'. *American Sociological Review*, 73: 854–73.

Kreyenfeld, M. and Hank, K. (1999), 'The availability of childcare and mothers' employment in West Germany'. DIW Discussion Paper, 191.

Krugman, P. (1991), 'History versus expectations'. *Quarterly Journal of Economics* (May): 651–67.

Kvist, J. (2002), 'Activating welfare states: How social policies can promote employment', in J. Clasen (ed.), *What Future for Social Security?* Bristol: The Policy Press, pp. 197–210.

Lam, D. (1997), 'Demographic variables and income inequality', in M. R. Rosenzweig and O. Stark (eds), *Handbook of Population and Family Economics*. Amsterdam: Elsevier Science, pp. 1015–59.

Lesthaege, Ron (1995), 'The second demographic transition in western countries: An interpretation', in K. Oppenheim Mason and A.-M. Jensen (eds), *Gender and Family Change in Industrialized Countries*. Oxford: Clarendon Press.

Levy, F. (1987), 'Dollars and dreams: The changing American income distribution'. New York: Russell Sage Foundation, pp. 160–6.

Levy, F. (1998), *The New Dollars and Dreams*. New York: Russell Sage.

Livi-Bacci, M. (2001), 'Comment: Desired family size and the future course of fertility'. *Population and Development Review*, 27 (supplement): 282–9.

Lucifora, C., McKnight, A. and Salverda, W. (2005), 'Low wage employment in Europe'. *Socioeconomic Review*, 3: 293–310.

Lundberg, S. (2005), 'Sons, daughters, and parental behavior'. *Oxford Review of Economic Policy*, 21: 340–56.

Lundberg, S. and Pollak, R. (2007), 'The American family and family economics'. *Journal of Economic Perspectives*, 21: 3–26.

Lundberg, S. and Rose, E. (2003), 'Child gender and the transition of marriage'. *Demography*, 40(2): 333–50.

Lundberg, S., McLanahan, S. and Rose, E. (2007), 'Child gender and father involvement in fragile families'. *Demography*, 44: 77–92.

Lundberg, S., Pollak, R. and Wales, T. (1997), 'Do husbands and wives pool their resources?' *Journal of Human Resources*, 32: 463–80.

Machin, S. and Vignoles, A. (2005), *What's the Good of Education?* Princeton: Princeton University Press.

Maitre, B., Whelan, C. and Nolan, B. (2003), 'Female partners' income contribution to the household income in the EU'. *EPAG Working Paper*, 43. Colchester: University of Essex.

Martin, M. A. (2006), 'Family structure and income inequality in families with children, 1976 to 2000'. *Demography* 43: 421–45.

Masnick, G. and Bane, M. J. (1984), *The Nation's Families*. Cambridge, MA: Auburn House Press.

Maurin, E. (2002), 'The impact of parental income on early schooling transitions'. *Journal of Public Economics*, 85: 301–32.

Mayer, K. U. (2004), 'Whose lives? How history, societies, and institutions define and shape life courses'. *Research in Human Development*, 13: 161–87.

Mayer, S. (1997), *What Money Can't Buy*. Cambridge, MA: Harvard University Press.

Mayers, M., Rosenbaum, D., Ruhm, C. and Waldvogel, J. (2004), 'Inequality in early childhood education and care: What do we know?', in K. Neckerman (ed.), *Social Inequality*. New York: Russell Sage, pp. 223–70.

McDonald, P. (2000), 'The tool-box of public policies to impact on fertility'. Paper presented at the *European Observatory on Family*, Sevilla (September 15–16).

McDonald, P. (2002), 'Low fertility:unifying the theory and the demography'. Paper presented at the *Population Association of America Meetings*, Atlanta, 9–11 May.

McLanahan, S. (2004), 'Diverging destinies: How children fare under the 2nd demographic transition'. *Demography*, 41: 607–27.

McLanahan, S. and Casper, L. (1995), 'Growing diversity and inequality in the American family', in R. Farley (ed.), *State of the Union: America in the 1990s*. New York: Russell Sage, pp. 1–45.

McLanahan, S. and Sandefur, G. (1994), *Growing up with a Single Parent*. Cambridge, MA: Harvard University Press.

Medina, L. (2005), 'The comparative statics of collective action'. *Rationality and Society*, 17: 423–52.

Mocan, H. (1995), 'Quality adjusted cost functions for child care centers'. *American Economic Review*, 85: 409–13.

Mocan, H. (1997), 'Cost functions, efficiency, and quality in day care centers'. *Journal of Human Resources*, 32: 861–91.

Mocan, H. (2007), 'Can consumers detect lemons? An empirical analysis of information asymmetry in the market for child care'. *Journal of Population Economics*, 20: 743–80.

Mooij, R. (2006), *Reinventing the Welfare State*. The Hague: Netherlands Bureau for Economic Policy Analysis.

Morris, M. and Western, B. (1999), 'Inequality in earnings at the close of the twentieth century'. *Annual Review of Sociology*, 25: 623–57.

Morrisette, R. and Johnson, A. (2004), 'Earnings of couples with high and low levels of education, 1980–2000'. Ottowa: Statistics Canada. Analytical Studies Research Paper Series, no. 230.

Musgrave, R. (1986), *Public Finance in a Democratic Society. Vol. II: Fiscal Doctrine, Growth and Institutions*. New York: New York University Press.

Myles, J. (2002), 'A new social contract for the elderly?' in G. Esping-Andersen, D. Gallie, A. Hemerijck and J. Myles, *Why We Need a New Welfare State*. Oxford: Oxford University Press, pp. 130–72.

Myles, J. (2003), 'Where have all the sociologists gone? Explaining economic inequality'. *Canadian Journal of Sociology*, 28: 553–61.

Neyer, G. (2003), 'Family policies and low fertility in Western Europe'. *Max Planck Institute for Demographic Research Working Paper*, 2003-021.

Nickell, S. (1997), 'Unemployment and labour market rigidities: Europe versus America'. *Journal of Economic Perspectives*, 11(3): 55–74.

Notestein, F. (1944), *The Future Population of Europe and the Soviet Union: Population Projections, 1940–1970*. Geneva: League of Nations.

Nyberg. A. (1994), 'The social construction of married women's labour force participation'. *Continuity and Change*, 9: 145–56.

Nygaard Christoffersen, M. (2004), *Familiens Udvikling I det 20ende Aarhundrede*. Copenhagen: SFI.

OECD (1996), *Caring for the Elderly*. Paris: OECD.

OECD (1997), *Literacy, Economy and Society*. Paris: OECD.

OECD (1998), *Maintaining Prosperity in Old Age*. Paris: OECD.

OECD (1999), *Employment Outlook*. Paris: OECD.

OECD (2000), *Literacy in the Information Age*. Paris: OECD.

OECD (2001), *A Caring World*. Paris: OECD.

OECD (2002), *Babies and Bosses. Reconciling Work and Family Life*. Vol. 1. Paris: OECD.

OECD (2003), *Knowledge and Skills for Life*. Paris: OECD.

OECD (2006), *Starting Strong II: Early Childhood Education and Care*. Paris: OECD.

OECD (2007), The OECD Family Database (*www.oecd.org/els/social/ family/database*).

Okonomisk Raad (2001), *Dansk Okonomi* (The Danish Economy). Copenhagen: Det Okonomiske Raads Formandsskab.

Oppenheimer, V. K. (1997), 'Women's employment and the gains to marriage'. *Annual Review of Sociology*, 23: 431–53.

Oxley, H., Dang, T., Forster, M. and Pellazari, M. (1999), 'Income inequalities and poverty among children and households with children in selected OECD countries'. Luxembourg: *LIS Working Paper Series*.

Pallier, B. (2002), *Gouverner la Sécurité Sociale*. Paris: Presses Universitaires de France.

Parsons, T. and Bales, R. (1955), *Family, Socialization and Interaction Processes*. Glencoe, IL: The Free Press.

Pasqua, S. (2001), 'Wives' work and income distribution in European countries'. *CHILD Working Paper* (June), University of Torino.

Pencavel, J. (1998a), 'Assortative mating by schooling and the work behaviour of wives and husbands'. *American Economic Review*, 88: 326–9.

Pencavel, J. (1998b), 'The market work behaviour and wages of women'. *Journal of Human Resources*, 38: 771–804.

Pencavel, J. (2006), 'Earnings inequality and market work in husband–wife families' (rev.), IZA Discussion Papers 2235, *Institute for the Study of Labor* (IZA).

Piketty, T. (2003), 'Theories of persistent inequality and intergenerational mobility', in A. B. Atkinson and F. Bourguignon (eds), *Handbook of Income Distribution*. Amsterdam: Elsevier, pp. 429–76.

Pissaridis, C., Garibaldi, P., Olivetti, C., Petrongolo, B. and Wasmer, E. (2003), *Women in the Labour Force: How Well is Europe Doing?* Report to the 5th European Conference of the Fondazione Debenedetti (Alghero, June).

Polacheck, S. (2003), 'How the human capital model explains why the gender wage gap narrowed'. *Maxwell School Working Paper*, no. 375, Syracuse University.

Polanyi, K. (1944), *The Great Transformation*. New York: Rinehart.

Polavieja, J. (2003), 'Temporary contracts and labour market segmentation in Spain'. *European Sociological Review*, 19(5): 501–18.

Pollak, R. A. (2005), 'Bargaining power in marriage: Earnings, wage rates and household production'. *NBER Working Paper*, 11239, March 2005.

Preston, P. (2004), 'The value of children', in D. Moynihan, T. Smeeding and L. Rainwater (eds), *The Future of the Family*. New York: Russell Sage, pp. 263–67.

Pryor, F. and Schaffer, D. (2000), *Who's not Working and Why?* Cambridge: Cambridge University Press.

Rainwater, L. and Smeeding, T. (2003), *Poor Kids in a Rich Country*. New York: Russell Sage.

Rake, K. (2000), *Women's Incomes over the Lifetime*. London: The Cabinet Office.

Raley, S., Mattingly, M. and Bianchi, S. (2006), 'How dual are dual earner couples?' *Journal of Marriage and Family*, 68: 11–28.

Ramey, V. (2006), 'A century of work and leisure'. *NBER Working Paper*, 12264.

Ramey, S. and Ramey, C. (2000), 'Early childhood experiences and developmental competence', in S. Danziger and J. Waldvogel (eds), *Securing the Future: Investing in Children from Birth to College*. New York: Russell Sage, pp. 122–50.

Reed, D. and Cancian, M. (2001), 'Sources of inequality: Measuring the contributions of income sources to rising family income inequality'. *Review of Income and Wealth*, 47: 302–21.

Rindfuss, R. (1991), 'The young adult years: Diversity, structural change, and fertility'. *Demography*, 28: 493–512.

Rosen, S. (1996), 'Public employment and the welfare state in Sweden'. *Journal of Economic Literature*, 34: 729–40.

Ruhm, C. (1998), 'The economic consequences of parental leave mandates'. *Quarterly Journal of Economics*, 113(1): 285–317.

Ruhm, C. (2004), 'Parental employment and child cognitive development'. *Journal of Human Resources*, 34: 155–92.

Ryscavage, P. (1999), *Income Inequality in America*. New York: M. E. Sharpe.

Ryscavage, P., Green, G. and Welniak, E. (1992), 'The impact of demographic, social, and economic change on the distribution of income'. *Journal of Income Distribution*, 12: 60–83.

Sarasa, S. (2004), 'El descenso de la natalidad y los servicios de proteccion social a los ancianos'. *Informacion Commercial Española*, 815: 205–18.

Sarasa, S. (2005), 'How do mid-life women reconcile adult care and employment?' Paper presented at ESPANET Conference, Friburg, September 25.

Sarasa, S. and Mestres, J. (2005), 'Women's employment and the adult caring burden'. *Demosoc Working Paper*, 7.

Sayer, L., Gauthier, A. and Furstenberg, F. (2004), 'Educational differences in parents' time with children: Cross-national variations'. *Journal of Marriage and the Family*, 66: 1152–69.

Schindler-Rangvid, B. (2006), 'Living and learning separately?' *AKF Working Paper*, February 4.

Schmid, G. (2008), *Full Employment in Europe*. Cheltenham: Edward Elgar.

Schokkaert, E. and Van Parijs, P. (2003), 'Social justice and the reform of Europe's pension systems'. *Journal of European Social Policy*, 13: 245–63.

Schrammel, K. (1998), 'Comparing the labor market success of young adults from two generations'. *Monthly Labor Review*, 121 (February): 3–9.

Schwartz, C. and Mare, R. (2005), 'Trends in educational assortative marriage from 1940–2003'. *Demography*, 42: 621–46.

Scott, J. (2008), 'Changing gender role attitudes', in J. Scott, S. Dex, and H. Joshi (eds), *Women and Employment: Changing Lives and New Challenges*. Cheltenham: Edward Elgar, pp. 156–78.

Shalev, M. (2008), 'Class divisions among women'. *Politics and Society*, 36: 421–44.

Shavit, Y. and Blossfeld, H. P. (1993), *Persistent Inequality: Changing Educational Attainment in Thirteen Countries*. Boulder: CO: Westview Press.

Shelton, B. and John, D. (1996), 'The division of household labor'. *Annual Review of Sociology*, 22: 299–322.

Sigle-Rushton, W. and Waldfogel, J. (2004), 'Family gaps in income: A cross-national comparison'. *Maxwell School of Citizenship and Public Affairs Working Paper*, 382.

Simonsen, M. (2005), 'Provision and costs of high quality day care and female employment'. Unpublished paper, Department of Economics, Aarhus University (April).

Sleebos, J. (2003), 'Low fertility rates in the OECD countries'. *OECD Social, Employment and Migration Working Paper*, 15.

Smeeding, T. (2004), 'Government programs and social outcomes: The United States in comparative perspective'. Paper presented at the Smolensky Conference, University of California, Berkeley (December 12–13).

Smith, M. (2005), 'Dual earning in Europe: Time and occupational equity'. *Work, Employment and Society*, 19: 131–9.

Soderstrom, M. and Uusitalo, R. (2004), 'School choice and segregation'. *IFAU Working Paper*, no. 7.

Solon, Gary (1999), 'Intergenerational mobility in the labor market', in Orley Ashenfelter and David Card (eds), *Handbook of Labor Economics*, Vol. 3A, Amsterdam: Elsevier Science, pp. 1761–1800.

Sorensen, A. and McLanahan, S. (1987), 'Married women's economic dependency, 1940–1980'. *American Journal of Sociology*, 93: 659–87.

Stevenson, B. and Wolfers, J. (2006), 'Bargaining in the shadow of the law'. *Quarterly Journal of Economics*, 121: 267–88.

Stier, L., Lewin-Epstein, N. and Braun, M. (2001), 'Welfare regimes, family supportive policies, and women's employment along the life course'. *American Journal of Sociology*, 106(6): 1731–60.

Storesletten, K. (2000), 'Sustaining fiscal policy through immigration'. *Journal of Political Economy*, 108(21): 300–23.

Thompson, L. (1998), *Older and Wiser: The Economics of Public Pensions*. Washington, DC: The Urban Institute.

UNICEF (2005), *A League Table of Child Poverty in Rich Countries*. Firenze: Innocenti Report Card.

US Census Bureau (1970), *Historical Statistics*. Washington, DC: The Census Bureau.

US Census Bureau (2005), *Current Population Reports*. Washington, DC: The Census Bureau.

US Census Bureau (2006), *Statistical Abstracts of the United States*. Washington DC: The Census Bureau.

Vaelfaerdskommissionen (2004), *Analyserapport.* Copenhagen: Velfaerdskommissionen.

Van de Kaa, D. (2001), 'Postmodern fertility preferences: From changing value orientation to new behavior'. *Population and Development Review*, 27 (supplement): 290–331.

Vandenbroucke, F. (2002), 'Foreword', in G. Esping-Andersen et al. (eds), pp. viii–xxiv.

Vleminckx, K. and Smeeding, T. (2001), *Child Well-being, Child Poverty and Child Policy in Modern Nations*. Bristol: Policy Press.

Waldfogel, J. (1998), 'Understanding the family gap in pay for women with children'. *Journal of Economic Perspectives*, 12: 137–56.

Waldfogel, J. (2002), 'Child care, women's employment and child outcomes'. *Journal of Population Economics*, 15: 527–48.

Waldfogel, J. and Mayer, S. (1999), 'Male–female differences in the low-wage labor market'. *JCPR Working Papers*, 70, Northwestern University/University of Chicago Joint Center for Poverty Research.

Waldfogel, J., Han, W. and Brooks-Gunn, J. (2002), 'The effects of early maternal employment on child cognitive development'. *Demography*, 39: 369–92.

Waldfogel, J., Higuchi, Y. and Abe, M. (1999), 'Family leave policies and women's retention after birth'. *Journal of Population Economics*, 12: 523–46.

Warren, J., Hauser, R. and Sheridan, J. (2002), 'Occupational stratification across the life course'. *American Sociological Review*, 67: 432–55.

Wasmer, E. (2002), 'The causes of the youth employment problem', in D. Cohen, T. Pikkety and G. Saint-Paul (eds), *The Economics of Rising Inequalities*. Oxford: Oxford University Press, pp. 133–46.

Western, B., Bloome, D. and Percheski, C. (2008), 'Inequality among American families with children: 1975–2005'. Unpublished manuscript. Harvard University, Kennedy School of Government.

Whelan, C., Layte, R. and Maitre, B. (2004), 'Understanding the mismatch between income poverty and deprivation: A dynamic comparative analysis'. *European Sociological Review*, 20: 287–302.

Wilkinson, R. (forthcoming), 'Inequality and health', in A. Giddens and P. Diamond, (eds), *The New Egalitarianism*. Cambridge: Polity.

Woessmann, L. (2004), 'How equal are equal opportunities? Family background and student achievement in Europe and the United States'. IZA Discussion Paper, no. 1284.

Wolfson, M., Rowe, G., Lin, X. and Gribble, S. (1998), 'Historical generational accounting with heterogeneous populations', in M. Corak (ed.), *Government Finances and Generational Equity*. Ottowa: Statistics Canada, pp. 107–26.

Wood, R. (1995), 'Marriage rates and marriageable men: A test of the Wilson hypothesis'. *Journal of Human Resources*, 30: 163–93.

Name Index

Subject Index